Let's Talk Pain

(Helping You To Discover Purpose In Suffering)

Cheryl Jones-Ross

Scriptures marked KJV are the King James Version, Public Domain.
"Italics in Scripture quotations have been added by the author for emphasis."
Library of Congress Cataloging-in-Publication Data

Names: Cheryl Jones-Ross. Author
(Let's Talk Pain)
Description:
Identifiers: LCCN 2019903315   ISBN (978-0-9986654-3-6)
Copyright © 2019 by (Cheryl Jones-Ross, Brtyca Publishing Company)

All rights reserved. No part of this book may be reproduced or transmitted in any form or by any means without written permission from the author.

CONTENTS

Chapter 1	Laying a Foundation For Your Life	Page 2
Chapter 2	Experiences, The Greatest Teacher	Page 8
Chapter 3	Now, Let's Talk Pain	Page 19
Chapter 4	The Importance Of Experiencing Pain	Page 34
Chapter 5	The Fruit Of Your Thoughts	Page 41
Chapter 6	Experiences, Biblically Speaking	Page 45
Chapter 7	Types Of Pain	Page 52
Chapter 8	Stages Of Labor	Page 63
Chapter 9	Growth, Development And The Wilderness	Page 73
Chapter 10	Rejection, The Road To Purpose	Page 82
Chapter 11	Abuse	Page 88
Chapter 12	I'm Over It	Page 93
Chapter 13	Dealing With Offences	Page 101
Chapter 14	Dis-Empower Your Past	Page 109
Chapter 15	Breaking Cycles	Page 116
Chapter 16	Know Your Worth	Page 119
Chapter 17	See The Beauty In Your Scars	Page 126

CHAPTER 1

Laying A Firm Foundation For Your Life

I Corinthians 3:10-11 says, "But let every man take heed how he buildeth thereupon. For other foundation can no man lay than that is laid, which is Jesus Christ".

The Lord has already laid a solid and a firm foundation for us to build on which is Jesus Christ, the word of God made flesh. If we are built up or are standing on anything other than the full gospel of Jesus Christ and "Him crucified", then we will not be able to stand the tests of time nor stand when trials and test come to discredit who we are and what we have been called by God to do.

We cannot get something for nothing in this life. Even King David understood that principal when he said, "*Nay; but I will surely buy it of thee at a price: neither will I offer burnt offerings unto the LORD my God of that which doth cost me nothing*". David needed God's favor because God was angry because David had numbered the people. He also understood that God's favor costs. Just as David did, we need to ask ourselves what price are we willing to pay for those opened doors, for "elevation" as we like to call it, and for fulfilled dreams and purposes.

Even though salvation is freely given, "*For by grace we are saved, through faith and that not of ourselves, it is the gift of God, not of works lest any man should boast*", we must also "*Take up our cross and follow Him*" and be willing to pay for purpose, with our lives if necessary.

"For which of you, intending to build a tower", the bible states. Meaning, if you purpose in your hearts to build an edifice, which is anything that you plan to do that will bring edification to the Lord, "*sitteth not down first, and counteth the cost, whether he have sufficient to finish it*"?

The Lord said, count the cost first, so that you will know if you have enough in you to get the job finished. That word sufficient in this scripture means, the goal or limit towards which movement is directed. This means that in order to discover if we have sufficient to finish what was began in us before the worlds were framed, we must ask these questions:

1. Where are we going with this?
2. How far are we going with it?
3. What is our goal and to what limit? (will we do xyz and abc or just xyz)
4. How are we going to get there (what is my part and what is your part in this mission)? Because we are workers together with Christ, He will not do it all and neither will He permit us to get all of the glory.
5. What is it going to take for me to accomplish that goal and take it as far as I can take it and then trust you to exceed my limitations. How much is this going to cost my life, and will I be able to trust Him when I can't understand or see the way that He wants me to go through?

If we are not willing to go the extent of what is required of us to complete what we plan to start, then we are doomed from the beginning. Therefore, it is vital that we have a clear understanding of what it will cost us to live a life of purpose so that we do not run to our destiny unprepared. Jesus said, *"Without me, you can do nothing"*. If our life is not centered in, rooted and grounded in Him, we walk this walk alone and our efforts will be in vain or useless.

Anything done without Him will yield no fruit that is useful for the kingdom of God. But, anything done in Christ and by the power of His word, will outlast time and even death. Therefore, a firm and sure foundation must be laid in a way that will ensure that the work will continue and live on even after we are long gone. If your thoughts are not towards leaving a legacy, an inheritance, and even leaving the essence of you in the hearts of people that you have poured into, then your work has been done in selfishness and not selflessness.

To accomplish this, it will be the amount of word power in you, how much of it you yield to, and how much of "you" dies in the process, that will determine if you reach the goal, how many people you will influence along the way and how great the thing will be that God is building in you.

- Will you reach tens, hundreds, thousands or millions?
- How large of a sphere of influence will you be given?
- Will you influence no one or will you have major impact on a few chosen ones who will take the work and build upon it?

For the answer to those questions, you will need to determine how much of you is already yielded to the word of God. You will know this by how well you currently handle situations that come into your life and how you have handled your past hurts and disappointments.

You will also need to know what is your current sphere of influence and then ask God what it will take for you to surpass that.

Then you must be willing to endure the effort that it will take to transform your life, as well as endure the sufferings that will accompany the process no matter how long it takes, or what it may cost you.

Let's begin by taking a short assessment of what is currently in your heart to do and figure out what it will take for you to go as far with it as you can go.

Name three things that are in your heart that you would like to do:

1._____

2._____

3._____

Name some obstacles in your own heart and mind that may hinder you from doing each of those things.

1._____
2._____
3._____
4._____
5._____

What initial actions will you have to take in order to deal with the hindrances in your life.

1._____
2._____
3._____
4._____

5._____

Now find a scripture that you can apply to each area of your life that needs work.

1._____
2._____
3._____
4._____
5._____

Everything begins with a foundation, whether it be a structure, ideologies, campaigns, ministries or personal development strategies. Even the things that are not clearly seen were founded upon the spoken word of God which is the greatest foundation that can be laid. Hebrews 11:3, *"Through faith we understand that the worlds were framed by the word of God, so that the things which are seen, were not made of things which do appear."*

It is imperative that you ask yourself:
- What am I standing on?
- What am I currently built upon?
- What is my life's purpose founded upon?
- Am I founded upon my own hopes and dreams?
- Am I what others have made me to be by what was passed down to me?
- Am I standing on the principles of my family, my environment or my own thought processes?
- Will my foundation be able to hold me up throughout the tests of time?"

The purpose of a foundation is to hold up and hold together the structure above it. A good and strong foundation keeps any edifice standing even when the forces of nature wreak havoc. In other words, it won't matter what the enemy brings in your life, nor how devastating the trouble is that you will have to walk through, if you have a good and strong foundation the essence of you will remain stable and standing once the storm has ended.

- A strong foundation not only keeps the edifice, but it also keeps the occupants of the building safe during calamities. Everything that the Lord has placed in you; purpose, destiny, His word, will remain safe and secure and undamaged in the time of great trials when the foundation has been built upon a solid rock.

- A good foundation must also be solid and sealed in a way that will keep water and moisture from seeping in and weakening the structure. If your foundation is free from cracks, it will keep the devil at bay as well as the effects of the world, and the trouble that the world brings out of your spirit and out of the will of God for your life.

According to construction experts and engineers, a foundation must be able to withstand the "dead" load and "live" loads.

- The dead load is the weight of the basic structure itself. This weight does not change as it supports the large vision, the mission, the teachings, the doctrine, and the fundamentals of the word of God in your life.

- The live load as it is called, is the weight of the people and all the things that they bring with them. These are the trials, the test, the offenses and the burdens of the lives of the people that have been connected to your life through birth, purpose and covenant relationships. Sometimes we have the burden of supporting other people in their trials while we are going through simultaneously. It is important to have a strong enough foundation so that you are not weakened when the time of crisis sweeps through you and your sphere of influence.

Laying a strong and a firm foundation takes time, effort and skill. You cannot start off right and then get off course by even a half of an inch. My pastor used to say, "If you start right and keep it right, it will end right". It is the little foxes that will spoil the vine!

We often ignore the little things that come into our lives that have the tendency to become great things down the road because we did not deal with it at the onset. This is why it is vital to work out any potential problems in your life early on or as soon as it happens, and not allow it to remain unattended to as it may cause a major catastrophe years later.

The Lord has designed a process to deal with potential problems that is sure to build a strong foundation. It will be through your growth and development phases that you will be made strong and firm for your destiny. We will talk more about growth and development later in this book.

Once a good and strong foundation has been laid through the growth and development phase of your life:

1. You will be perfected - Complete, mature.
2. You will be stablished - Firm, constant, and stable.
3. You will be strengthened - Confirmed in knowledge and power.
4. You will be settled - Standing on a firm foundation.

It is important to understand that the Lord is building something different in each one of us. Therefore, the time, the effort, and the process needed to build in me will be far different from what is needed to build a firm foundation in you. We are not all going the same place nor are each of us created for the same purpose and mission. We cannot look at others as the blueprint for what the Lord will do in our lives according to where we are going.

What we are going to be building on top of the foundation will also determine how long it will take for the foundation to be completed. This process cannot be rushed or taken lightly. If we refuse to develop patience and learn how to rest in what the Lord is doing in us during this foundational phase, we will be unsteady, unstable and constantly wavering in our faith.

There are many who are operating in the Kingdom of God who are unstable because of a rocky foundation. They are emotionally, spiritually and mentally unbalanced because they did not take the time that was needed to properly build them up.

You must go through the experiences that have been designed for your life and quickly learn the lessons that each experience brings so that you can be prepared for every good work".

As a part of the foundational phase, the Lord has created times, seasons, eras, dispensations and even days for us to go through experiences that were designed to teach us the lessons that we must learn for stability and functionality.

CHAPTER 2

Experiences, The Greatest Teacher

The Lord, who is in the dateless pass as well as in the dateless future at the same time, has marked out time for the benefit of mankind. These time spans created by God in the beginning when He created the sun and the moon, were designed so that we will learn how to operate within certain parameters and to teach us how to reach goals and complete assignments in a timely manner. Even though the Lord is eternal, man only has a certain amount of time to do what he was placed on this earth to do and it must be done in alignment with the universal plan of God. However, the most important increment of time that we have been given to work within is days.

Psalms 90:10 says, *"the days of our years are threescore years and ten; and if by reason of strength they be fourscore years yet is their strength labour and sorrow; for it is soon cut off, and we fly away"*. If we really take note of this passage and begin to see the number of years that we have been given as days, our days would amount to approximately 25,550 days that we have been given to spend on destiny and purpose.

Time is to be spent, but not wastefully, nor is it to be squandered. Time is extremely valuable and once it is used up, there is no more time for us to spend.

Even though this scripture lets us know that a certain amount of days has been given to us by promise, some die sooner while others live to eighty or longer if the body is strong. Even if we make it to the end of those seventy or eighty years, the bible says that the best of those years was filled with pride, mischief, pain, grief, iniquity, vanity, emptiness and sorrow and soon those years disappear, and we fly away. At the end of most of our lives we will most certainly find ourselves asking, "where did all of that time go"?

I compare time to having two hundred dollars in your purse and spending most of it in the course of a day and looking at what you have left wondering what you spent all that money on. You may start looking at your receipts and realize how much money you spent on a pair of shoes, or on snacks, and hair products, and then wishing that you had more money to spend on what you really needed. However, life has no receipts that help you to keep track of where all of your time went. You may find yourself in your sixties looking back at what you did in your thirties and realizing all the time you wasted. But the sad truth may be that you will not know what you did with every single day of it.

Years don't really matter as much to us when we are young. While in our twenties, we think that we have time in abundance. We waste those years living in sin, un-forgiveness, anger, bitterness, resentment, sick, poor, weak, and failing to learn lessons from our experiences. When we are young, we think we have all the time in the world, so we make snap decisions and live for the moment with little thought of the long term consequences for our immediate gratifications.

Just as we must learn how to be good stewards over all that we have been given, we must also learn how to manage our time and make wise investments with the days that we have been given while we are yet young. Ephesians 5:15 says, *"See then that ye walk circumspectly, not as fools, but as wise, Redeeming the time, because the days are evil"*. Time was given to you to be used to invest in your life's mission and not used to do as you wish.

We are to:
- regulate our time with accuracy.
- make wise and sacred use of every opportunity to do good despite whatever it is that we may be experiencing at the moment.

Psalms 90:11-12 says, *"Who knoweth the power of thine anger? even according to thy fear, so is thy wrath, so teach us to number our days, that we may apply our hearts unto wisdom"*.

Teach us how to number our days, not count them, but assign a number on the days that we are living in. We must begin to train our minds to understand that, "this is day number 21,170 of my life and I must make wise decisions about what to do with this day".

We must begin to be intentional in our assessment of what we did with each day. At the end of our days we will have to give an accurate report of what we have done with the Lord's time. We will also be expected to:
- prove our profitability and good stewardship.

- use the things that come in our lives to increase our chances of success or effectiveness (being successful in producing a desired or intended result).
- have found ways to grow, to increase, to be of a benefit to the kingdom of God, to the mission of God and to the body of Christ.

To begin your assessment, make a list of everything that you did yesterday that you believe was productive:

_____
_____
_____
_____
_____
_____
_____
_____
_____

Now make a list of your five greatest accomplishments within the past year:

_____
_____
_____
_____
_____
_____
_____

We belong to God; we are His servants. As a matter of fact, the word says, *"For ye are bought with a price: therefore glorify God in your body, and in your spirit, which are God's".* That word glorify means to cause the dignity and the worth of God to become manifest and acknowledged.

Well how do we do this? The Lord gives us opportunities each and every day for us to show forth His dignity and His worth, to make Him desirable, useful and valuable to others and to advance the kingdom of God. All are given opportunities; however all will not have the same zeal or determination to take advantage of or more importantly maximize the opportunities.

The scripture says that the Lord God called his (own) servants, those who were already busy working for the kingdom. He gave different amounts to different servants. *"And unto one he gave five talents, to another two, and to another one; to every man according to his several ability;"* or his own power or influence.

Talents are not natural ability, but God gives talents based on our ability to gain increase. This is why the bible says, *"to whom much is given, much is required"*. All are not given the same amount of talents as clearly stated in the text.

A talent is something that can be invested, traded, and risked with the possibility of gain or loss. Whenever something is invested, it is expected to produce a return. When you make an investment, you are looking for some sort of benefit even though you understand that there is a risk in investing that can lead to loss.

Whenever opportunities come to use our abilities and invest our talents, we understand that we are taking a chance. But regardless of whatever the risks are, whatever situation that may interject itself to jeopardize the plan, we still expect to have a favorable result. In other words, the risks will never outweigh the opportunity to make good use of the Lord's time.

Make a list of opportunities for advancement that you have passed over in the past year and list the reason why you did or did not take advantage of that opportunity.

Opportunity	Why/Why not
_____	_____
_____	_____
_____	_____
_____	_____

I took nearly every opportunity that came my way to use my gifts and abilities over the years. Some of those opportunities worked in my favor, others did not. Please understand that I was not an opportunist meaning, I was not a person who exploited circumstances or opportunities to gain an advantage. An opportunist is not in it for the long haul, nor do they care about the plan or the mission. They are not willing to suffer in order to gain anything. But they have their own agenda and seize the opportunity to advance themselves and then they are out with the least amount of risk. I however, understood the importance of seizing the moment and maximizing the opportunities that were presented to me and I suffered loss along the way.

An opportunity is also a favorable or advantageous circumstance or a combination of circumstances. Whenever a circumstance is favorable, that means it can be accepted. It shouldn't matter when the opportunity comes or what form it comes in, or even if it will cause us pain, it is still favorable, and we should accept it and take advantage of it. But only if it:

- Lines up with your purpose and destiny.
- Will give God glory and advance His kingdom?
- Agrees with the word of God.
- The risk is not to your character or integrity.
- The risk does not cause intentional harm to others.

Always be mindful that each opportunity is an opportunity to learn, to gain experience, to set ourselves up for another opportunity, even if we fail. Failure will eventually lead to success because of what you will learn through the failure.

In the passage we see that the man with two talents had gained two talents more. Did he fail in that he did not produce as much as the man with five talents? No. He was just as successful. He did not waste opportunities to use his gifts even though he may not have had as many abilities as the other man. He also took a risk and was equally committed to gain. However, the third servant had one talent and the bible says, *"he took it and buried it in the ground"*. Because of this, his master called him an unprofitable servant. Why? Because, he was so afraid to take a risk that he did nothing, he gained nothing, he profited nothing.

It will take wisdom to know how to navigate through the risk. The unprofitable servant did not use wisdom but made decisions according to his feelings. He allowed fear, slothfulness and a lack of understanding to keep him from being productive.

Wisdom is not just the ability to make right decisions, but wisdom encompasses our ability to be creative in working the plan of God. It is our God given creativity that helps us to figure out how to do or make something new and something valuable in order to complete the assignment. It causes us to intentionally expose ourselves to new experiences, new situations, and greater knowledge.

Let's talk a little about your level of creativity. Circle *yes* or *no* to answer each of the following questions.

- Have you ever had an original idea? Yes   No
- Have you ever solved a problem that no one else could? Yes   No
- Have you ever moved quickly on an idea that you have had? Yes   No
- Are you a deep thinker? Yes   No
- Are you a daydreamer? Yes   No
- Do you love a challenge? Yes   No
- Have you ever re-purposed an item? Yes   No
- I hate problems. Yes   No
- I am self-motivated? Yes   No
- I do my best work with detailed directions. Yes   No
- I do my best work figuring it out on my own. Yes   No
- I am a self-starter. Yes   No
- I can keep myself motivated without outside stimulus. Yes   No
- I can focus on a project until it is completed. Yes   No
- I love to do research. . Yes   No
- I would rather wing-it? Yes   No

Visit my website at www.cheryljonesross.com and click on the tab "The Let's Talk Community" for more information on discovering your creativity.

Wisdom is also skill and dexterity in use of the word of God in bringing the plan to pass in the time that we have been given.

Here are some ways in which we need to begin to apply wisdom in our lives on a daily basis:

•In administration – We must know how to manage our lives and live our life daily with plans and goals. Anything done without a plan risks failure. Even though we may learn from failure, we do not plan to fail. Therefore, we must get control of our own lives with good management! See where your time is going and decide what is productive use and what is wasteful and then live accordingly.

•In skill in war - We must remember that we are in a battle daily, but the battle is in our minds against an enemy that we cannot see who suggests thoughts and ideas that are contrary to God's thoughts and to His word. You must know who the real enemy is, a devil with a diabolical scheme to steal your time with distractions that take away your focus.

- In prudence in religious affairs - We must learn how to behave ourselves daily with wisdom and grace so that we do not become an embarrassment to the kingdom. If we do not learn how to handle the affairs of our lives, we will mismanage the assignment when it comes to us. It is also vital that we understand that if we are not faithful over that of another man's, the Lord will not give us our own to be faithful to.

- In dexterity - We need skill, quickness, readiness and awareness every day of our lives so that we will know how to be crafty in winning souls. The bible says, *"he that winneth souls is wise"*. Everything is not always about you; your call is to people who must be dealt with in a way that is relevant to who they are and where they are going in their lives too.

- In keeping our wits - We must always learn how to be sober and vigilant and stay calm and collected at every moment in the day. If we have not mastered our emotions, we cannot master our ministry. Peace and patience will be two of your greatest tools in exercising self-control, however one is given to you, while the latter comes by way of the process.

Many of the experiences that we must go through, have the potential to be time wasters, if we allow ourselves to get "stuck" in them. We must quickly discern what to do when we are faced with "risky" situations. These are situations that have the ability to waste time and steal your focus.

In the book of Joel 2:25 the Lord talks about the stages in the life of a locust, one of the greatest devourers of crops that has been created. Crops are representative of growth, fruit and production in our lives. The locust comes into your life in different stages and seasons bringing with it four types of experiences that you must be exposed to. We can call these experiences risks.

Let's briefly look at these different types of "insects ".

1. The locust: meaning sudden disappearance. This speaks of the losses in our life and the time that we have wasted with regrets over the things that we have lost, lost dreams, the loss of a loved one through death or divorce, the loss of possessions or a job or even our own peace and joy.

    Our stance towards loss can lead to long periods of grief, regret, disappointment and even anger if not properly dealt with. We must learn how to correctly identify and discern the purpose of people, conditions and situations that come in our lives in a proper manner so that we are not devastated over the temporary things that we mistook for permanence.

Every condition is not in our lives to stay and neither is everyone that comes into our lives there to stay. Some are sent to help us through a certain time period or condition, others are with us all the way through to our purpose and destiny, and some are sent as time wasters.

There are also circumstances and conditions that come in our lives situationally or permanently. If we mistake something for permanence that was only sent as an experience for growth and maturity, we may fall into the trap of wasting time trying to restore something that the Lord has planned to do away with.

2. The cankerworm: the devourer. This speaks of the things that have the potential to overwhelm or consume you. Perhaps you have a child that is engulfed in addiction, or you are dealing with a wayward spouse, or struggling for years living in lack. These are overwhelming situations that will consume your time as you try to figure out how to "fix" a problem that may not be yours to fix.

There are certain things that are allowed in our lives to teach us how to pray and to show us how-to live-in peace so that we are not overwhelmed. There are also certain conditions in our lives in which we must simply learn how to be content in. The bible says that *"Godliness with contentment is great gain"*.

The word godliness in this passage means holiness. But it also means reverence and respect towards God. Reverence and respect towards God with contentment is great gain. Meaning, this will cause us to carry or move forward, and to bring about or to procure for one's self. In other words, godliness with contentment is how we get to our "next" from the situations that are overwhelming.

Paul said in Philippians 4:11, *"Not that I speak in respect of want"*. He was saying apart from the things that I want, *"I have learned, in whatsoever state I am, therewith to be content"*. I have learned to be independent of my external circumstances by separating my inner man from those external circumstances so that I can be alright no matter what is happening in my life.

He went on to say, *"I know both how to be abased, and I know how to abound"*. I know how to bring myself low through humble living and I also know how-to live-in abundance. He said, *"everywhere and in all things, I am instructed both to be full and to be hungry"*. I have learned to be satisfied and to eagerly desire more at the same time and not let either condition affect the other!

What a place of contentment to be in.

He also said, I have learned *"both to abound and to suffer need"*. I know how to live when I have overflow and when I am in want, or when I am lacking and not let either condition affect my joy, my worship, my faith because, *"I can do all things through Christ which strengtheneth me"*.

3. The caterpillar: the revenger: These experiences are the ones that we generally refuse to accept responsibility for. This is when we are afflicted in response to the hurt that we inflicted upon others. We must clearly understand that we reap what we sow in every area of our lives.

Many of us are suffering by someone who has hurt us in word, deed or action. But how many of us have asked the Lord to reveal to us why we are experiencing this type of pain?

Offences will come, we will never escape being offended or hurt by people. (We will talk more in-depth about offences later in this book). In the meantime, it is imperative that we understand that not only will we reap what we have sown into the lives of others but, we will reap it at the same level of pain that we sowed it into someone else's life. We will be allowed to hurt the way we hurt them and cry in the way that we caused others to cry. We will not be able to escape the law of reciprocity. This is one good reason for us to be careful how we treat others.

And yet, God is merciful and will pardon and show mercy to those of us who quickly learn the lesson and ask for forgiveness from Him and when warranted, forgiveness from those that we have knowingly hurt.

Be quick to forgive, be longsuffering and forbearing of one another. Remember, love never fails. This does not mean that we will not reap what we have sown if we do these things, however, we can lean on the mercy of God who, if He so chooses, can reduce the time in which we have to experience the revenger in our lives.

4. The palmerworm: to be pulled to pieces. The devil does not always come at us all at once. But his intention is to slowly wear us down with the things that we think that we can't do anything about. These are the problems that stay in our lives for a long period of time without an end in sight, zapping us of energy and strength to fight. Jesus said to Peter. " *Simon, Simon, behold Satan hath desired to have you that he may sift you as wheat, But I have prayed for thee that thy faith fail not and when thou art converted, strengthen thy brethren*".

    When we are weak, it is hard to get up and move. Some of us have been stuck in situations for many years, because our mind and our faith have been made weak from years of staying in that condition. The only way to overcome this type of weakness is to get up and do something about our situation. We will discuss this more in the chapter, "I'm Over It".

I love how the Lord gives a solution to our wasting of precious time over the years. In Joel 2:25, the Lord said, *"And I will restore to you the years that the locust hath eaten, the cankerworm, and the caterpillar, and the palmerworm, my great army which I sent among you"*. In this passage the Lord is saying, as soon as you allow these things to do in you what I have sent them to do, which is to train you, mature you and prepare you, *"I will restore the years"*. He did not say that he would restore things, conditions, or bring back people in our lives, but He said the years that these experiences took from our life.

I was in my fifties when I planted Greater Hope Restoration Ministries after thirty-six years of being faithful in a previous ministry. During my first year as the new Senior Pastor (I served in leadership fifteen years prior to that), I would often ask the Lord why He waited so long to bring me into my purpose. However, I was never waiting on Him, but He was orchestrating my life so that I could learn the valuable lessons that I would need to fulfill the mission. Because it took me so long to "get it", it also took what I thought was a long time for me to be ready for what He had planned for my life all along.

And yet in that time that I was wasting, He had prepared a people who would need what I had gone through and overcame, people that I could freely pour into whose lives would rapidly be changed. This is an example of how all things work together for good.

It wasn't until I began to move in the perfect will of God, that I realized that I was not ready for what the Lord had for me at the time that I wanted it to happen. I spent years in my "teenage" stage of growth believing that I knew everything and that I was mature enough to handle the responsibility of the lives of the people of God, when I knew nothing at all.

However, when I began to yield to God's perfect will, which previously went against what I wanted, what I knew, and what I was willing to risk or give up to have it, the Lord began to accelerate the lessons so that I arrived at my destination at the appointed time.

When I accepted what the Lord wanted to do, I found myself doing things within our ministry in a few short years that it has taken other churches years to get to. Our ministry quickly grew from a handful to two hundred plus in less than three years through a major impact from outreach in the communities. Since my release to ministry in 2014, I have also written four books, launched a television ministry and a successful magazine as well as become a relevant voice in the lives of people struggling to find purpose in pain.

Many are running to do ministry but have not allowed themselves to be trained and matured through the process of time. Therefore, they are not able to handle the assignment and find themselves unstable, quitting or even continuing all the while struggling with internal conditions that tarnish the effectiveness of their work.

However, if you allow yourself to stay in the process of time, you will not arrive any sooner than necessary, neither will you be too late, as long as you learn the lessons that accompany experiences.

CHAPTER 3

Now, Let's Talk Pain

The most common reason why people seek help from the medical profession is because they want to get rid of some type of pain. And one of the most common reasons why people come to Jesus is because they want to get rid of some type of pain.

Physical pain, emotional, and spiritual pain are all similar in many ways, in that each lets us know that something is not functioning in us according to God's design for our body, soul and spirit.

Pain is not God's way of punishing us for our mistakes or making us suffer because we deserve it. But pain is merely an indicator that:

- There is an issue in our lives that must be addressed.
- We are on the verge of coming into a new season in our lives.
- We are about to birth the purpose that the Lord has ordained for our lives.
- We are being made to suffer for Jesus' name sake.
- There are lessons that we must learn to equip us for where we are going.

All pain in our lives is not an indicator of sin in our lives, but all pain has a source or a root cause that must be identified so that it can be dealt with. Pain also has a purposed driven cause that will always work for good in our lives.

The beauty of it all is that the Lord will never allow any condition, circumstance or type of suffering to come into our life that we are not already equipped to withstand. He already knows what is in us, and He knows us better than we do. He knows the condition of our hearts and exactly what type of trials and test are necessary for our lives to cause our hearts to be pliable enough to become willing and available vessels.

Even though we must suffer, it is still God's will that we prosper and be in health, even as our souls prosper and that we are made whole in every area of our lives. That phrase *"every whit whole"* found in John 7:23 means, to be completely sound in body, to be healthy and not deviating from the truth of the teaching and instructions of Jesus who has come to not just set you free, but make you free indeed. There is a real difference in being set free and made free, even though we are made to exist in both conditions. When we are made free, we have been manumitted, meaning:

a. We have been set free from captivity and its effects on our lives.
b. We have been freed from the hand or the control of our captor which was the devil.
c. We have been permanently loosed from restraints and all the things that can bind, confine, entangle or oppress us.

When one is set free, there is a possibility of future confinement or restraint. There is no permanent state of liberation because the enemy's power has not been broken over your life.

Hence the need for manumission or the act of the master voluntarily freeing the slave. This act was often written into the will of the master of a slave. The freedom of the slave was an intentional act that was predetermined by the master. Therefore, it could not be altered or revoked. It was always the plan of God who is not only our master, but our friend, to guarantee our freedom through Jesus way before the worlds were framed. It was then that He adopted a plan by His word to ensure that we are no longer under the oppression of the devil and his plans and schemes to keep us enslaved to sin and the effects of sin in the world.

We may be thinking, if we have been freed from bondage and oppression, why must we endure sufferings and hardships. Should not our lives be that of eating, drinking and being merry on a continuous basis? After all, Jesus paid the price for our freedom with His life.

This is the thought process of many people. We believe that once we begin to make positive changes in our lives, that all our sufferings should come to an end. And once we begin to experience trouble in our new lives, we want to return from whence we came believing that the trouble that we experience has no value. The Children of Israel wanted to go back to Egypt, their place of enslavement, when they began to experience what seemed to them as even more hardships in the wilderness than what they had been set free from in Egypt.

But hardships, sufferings, difficulties, trials and pain will always be valuable no matter where we came from or where we are going. Job said, *"man that is born of a woman is of a few days and full of trouble"*. Trouble is coming no matter how good we think we are and no matter how wonderful of a relationship we have with the Lord. And once we begin to see pain and suffering for what it really is, our friend, we will begin to embrace its process in our lives with a clear understanding of its value, relevance and purpose.

So, calm down, BREATHE, and by all means, LIVE. This same God that has freed you, knows how to keep you free from bondages and He knows what is best for you. He already made you of a substance that can endure the pressure of pain and come out of it better and not bitter. Therefore, you will survive it!

Numbers 31:22, 23 says, *"Only the gold the silver the brass the iron, the tin and lead. Everything that may abide the fire, ye shall make it go through the fire and it shall be clean. Nevertheless it shall be purified with the water of separation: and all that abideth not the fire ye shall make go through the water"*. Meaning, if you are in it, it is because you are made of a substance that can take the heat and not die in the furnace of afflictions. So, rejoice, you are of a precious component made to withstand any and every trial or test that may come your way.

But more importantly, the test will not last forever. The bible says, *"with the temptation"*, meaning the trial of your fidelity, integrity, virtue and constancy, *"the Lord will also make a way to escape so that you will be able to bear it"*. There is an exit, but the exit will only come once you have been taught the necessary lesson that you must learn through your experiences, and it will come when you have had enough of your condition to do something about it.

The bible clearly teaches of a way of escape from our afflictions when it speaks of the man that sat by the pool of Bethesda for thirty-eight long years. This impotent man at the pool understood that an angel was to come at a season to "trouble the water" which would have been his way of escape out of his condition. However, he did not take the exit, but made excuses as to why he could not get in the water at any particular season and stayed in bondage for many years.

Here are some necessary truths concerning pain that you must come to understand so that you can progress in your life and not get stuck in the pain as that man did for all of those years.

1. Pain is good for you.

No one wants to suffer, and when trials come, we focus on finding that exit door so that we can quickly get out of it. Even though the condition is meant to be temporary, you must allow the time allotted for it to work in your life. One way to help you to go through is to understand that the pain is good for you. Psalms 119:71, King David said, *"It is good for me that I have been afflicted, that I may learn your statues"*.

So, what was David saying in this passage of scripture? He was saying exactly what is written, the trouble is good! In this passage he was not saying that trouble feels good, because it never feels good to be in pain, unless you suffer from some sort of condition that makes you enjoy being in pain, but that phrase "good for me" means that the affliction was:

1. Agreeable to my spiritual senses.
2. Valuable to my purpose.
3. A benefit to my life.
4. And it: Ushered me into God's best for my life.

2. Pain is a teaching tool in that it:

a. It trains us in the word of God.
b. Makes us an expert through experiences.
c. Teaches us how to be skillful in spiritual matters.
d. Teaches us who God is.

That phrase "Your Statutes" means, the prescribed task or portion of what the Lord has endorsed or authorized for your life. The Lord wants results, but He is expecting to get right results. Right results can only be produced through the process of sanctification and purification, by a prescribed procedure, by a particular action, or course. There is a particular procedure that you must go through that has been prescribed by the Lord so that your life will go a particular way, so that He will get an outcome that will give Him the right results.

When something is prescribed that means:

a. It is ordered.
b. It has been laid down as a guide, direction, or rule of action.

Psalms 37:23 says, *"The steps of a good man are ordered by the LORD: and he delighteth in his way"*. This means that his way has been:

a. Established
b. Prepared
c. Arranged
d. Settled

The prescribed procedure for our life is different for every single one of us. You will not have to overcome some of the things that I have had to overcome, and I won't have to deal with some of the things that you are going to have to deal with. But the process that you will have to go through will be necessary for you and you alone. You can't compare your life, your walk, your process to somebody else's because God is doing something new and distinct in you through it.

That word process means: A series of actions, changes, or functions bringing about a result. In the process, there will be a series of actions that occur in your life, a number of events that seem to be arranged to come one after the other in succession. These will be things that God uses to sanctify and purify you and get all of those unfavorable and undesirable traits, faults, thoughts and sins out of you.

It was the series of actions, changes and functions (the process) that taught David how to take the limits off the Lord. Many of us have limitations on God because we have not experienced Him in the fulness of who He is and of what He is able to do in and for us. We experienced His blessings, the warmth of His presence, His grace and His mercy in our lives and all the benefits that He gives us when we come into relationship with Him. However, we will never really know Him in all His ways until we have experienced Him through fellowship or being associated with His sufferings.

Paul said, *"That I might know Him in the power of His resurrection and in the fellowship of His sufferings"*. Paul wanted to understand God not just through relationship by way of the resurrection power of Christ, but also by participation in the afflictions, hardships and pain that Christ endured for our sakes.

He was saying, "I don't just want to know Him, but I want to know Him in a suffering way, in a way that causes me to have to suffer in order to grow, to produce and to be useful in the kingdom and in a way that causes me to die to myself so that He is all that is alive in me".

3. Pain works patience.

The bible says, *"Therefore we glory in tribulations also: knowing that tribulation worketh patience; And patience, experience; and experience, hope: And hope maketh not ashamed; because the love of God is shed abroad in our hearts by the Holy Ghost which is given unto us"*.

Patience is not brought about by dealing with people, that is longsuffering. Neither is patience an action, but it is a character trait. It is the characteristic of a man who has not swerved from his deliberate purpose and his loyalty to faith even by the greatest of trials and sufferings.

Let's look at some truths about patience:
  a. Patience is the instrument that the Lord uses to help us to get our mind under control.
  b. Patience shuts down the plans and schemes of the unregenerate mind and causes the flesh and the body to line up with the word of God and His plan for our life.
  c. Patience causes us to keep going even when the flesh is saying, "I quit".
  d. Patience is that "can do" mind, that *"I can do all things through Christ that strengthens me"* mind.
  e. Patience causes us, by the word of God, to change our perception about our situation.
  f. Patience settles our spirit man so that we will allow the experiences that trouble brings about to perfect us and cause us to bear fruit at the appointed time.
  g. Patience is not the ability to wait, but it is the end result of a test.
  h. Patience is steadfastness and constancy.
  i. Patience is the ability to accept or tolerate unfavorable conditions or endure suffering without being affected by it.

The bible says that we must, *"Let patience have her perfect work"*. Meaning we must:

      a. Let patience have her complete work.

        b. Let her have her conclusion of the matter.

      c. Let her work out our maturity.

"That ye may be perfect and entire, wanting nothing".

    a.   That you may be complete.

    b.   That God's work in you may be concluded.

    c.   So that you may come to full age.

    d.   So that you may be whole in every area of your life.

    e.   So that you won't have lack in any area of your life.

4. Pain conditions our minds.

Pain is a conditioner for our minds once we learn how to properly fight the good fight of faith.

That word condition means: To bring (something) into the desired state for use. We must condition our own minds just as an athlete conditions himself for a competition. Paul said in 1 Corinthians 9:27 in the amplified bible, *"But [like a boxer] I buffet my body [handle it roughly, discipline it by hardships] and subdue it"*. What Paul was saying was, " I have already prepared myself before the fight began by hitting my own self in the face and body. By doing this, I conditioned myself to keep from flinching when the blows came.

When one flinches that means that he/or she makes a quick, nervous movement of the face or body by instinctive reaction to surprise, fear or pain. An instinctive reaction is an innate and typically fixed pattern of behavior in response to certain actions. It is an innate pattern of behavior to flinch when one is expecting something that is coming in their direction to cause pain or injury. However, if we flinch at the devil's attacks, he will use our reaction against us in order to build a strategy in his fight against us.

Paul said in 1 Corinthians 9:26, *"I therefore so run, not as uncertainly (or with lack of confidence); so fight I, not as one that beateth the air"*. He was saying, I know what to fight, when to fight, how to fight, where to fight and I know who my real opponent is, I know his tactics and I have prepared myself with a pre-fight strategy.

Most of us are spending all our power and energy fighting the wrong fight. We waste time fighting with people, situations, circumstances not realizing that we are not wrestling with flesh and blood. Or, we go to the opposite end of the spectrum and see every adverse situation as spiritual warfare. If somebody upsets us, we go to blows, if our car breaks down, we start swinging at demons, if our spouse doesn't meet up to our expectations we are casting the devil out of him or her, if something happens on our job we take the oil to work and fling it on everyone's desk and begin binding the devil all the while wasting time and energy fighting the things that God has not sanctioned or approved us to fight.

Jeremiah 12:5 says, "*If thou hast run with the footmen, and they have wearied thee, then how canst thou contend with horses? and if in the land of peace, wherein thou trustedst, they wearied thee, then how wilt thou do in the swelling of Jordan*"? What God was saying to Jeremiah is, if the little things that come in your life make you whine and complain so much, how will you react when you become faced with much greater from enemies much more powerful than what you are currently dealing with?

We are spending our lives dealing with little things. "*It's the little foxes that spoil the vine. A little leaven leaveneth the whole lump*". It is these little things that we are contending with that are wearing us out before we can even get to the real fight. While we are wearing out from the insignificant issues, the enemy, who has a strategy, is coming in the house taking our stuff because the strong man is preoccupied fighting a fight that has no relevance in his life. Luke 11:21 says, "*When a strong man armed keepeth his palace, his goods are in peace:*".

What must you do in order to defeat him?
      a. Get a pre-fight strategy.
      b. Follow the plan of action from the Lord.
      c. Know your adversary.
      d. Protect yourself. Keep the enemy from landing punches that have the potential to knock you out.
      e. Be willing to wait for the right time to attack. Remember, patience may be your greatest strategy.
      f. Be sober, keep your mind right!

As I stated earlier, every event is not a spiritual battle, but when one comes, you will know that these things are not your normal fight. If you are not careful, you won't recognize where the attack originated from and you will try to fight these spiritual fights in the same way that you have always fought carnal battles or natural occurrences in your life.

However, a spiritual fight requires weapons that are spiritual because you are no longer fighting what you can see, what you can hear and feel. You may be used to using excuses, blaming, bitterness, rage, unforgiveness, lying, partial truths, cunningness, mouth running, complaining, murmuring, crying, pity, manipulation, cussing people out and the list could go on and on as your weapons of choice.

But, that won't work against the devil because the devil is not impressed with nor moved by your carnality. So, in order to be victorious, you must learn how to get out of your flesh and fight in a place that you know nothing about with enemies that are invisible and out to kill you.

The devil doesn't fight fair. He comes after your hopes and dreams, he comes after your loved ones, your possessions, your body, your mind, your peace, your joy and he is sneaky and cunning and tactical and does it in a way that causes you to not even think that it is him. Nine times out of ten, he is the last one that you will blame or accuse for the wrong doings that happen in your life. He is a deceptive, divisive liar who paints the lie as the truth and tries to turn the truth into the lie.

Therefore, you must be:
- Sober, meaning be calm and watch (an act or instance of carefully observing things over a period of time).
- Be vigilant, be actively cautious.
- Take heed because your adversary the devil as a roaring lion, walketh about seeking whom he may devour, destroy, swallow up.

He seeks, meaning he makes do use of opportunities to plot against you. A plot is a plan made in secret by a group of people to do something illegal or harmful. Everything that he does is illegal and harmful and his plot is with intent, with an objective, a goal to devour you. But you don't have to take what he tries to do to you.

You may ask how do I contend or deal with an enemy that I can't see?

- When you deal with your adversary, you take action to do something to solve the problem, to put him to flight, and cause the right results to be produced in spite of the wrong inflicted. (You will see throughout most of this book you will be prompted to do something about your life and you will also be instructed on how to begin, however, the actual doing will be up to you).

- Fight with intensity (strength, power and force).
- Fight with a purpose, with determination and tirelessness.
- You assert. Meaning you cause the enemy to recognize your authority or rights) by confident and forceful behavior.
- Maintain control of yourself at all times.
- You hold on to the promises of God for your life.
- Claim what is yours. Even if you have to argue with yourself until yourself lines up with the word of God.
- Insist that the devil take his hands off your stuff.
- You state the facts and not suppositions (speculations, feelings, hunches, ideas).
- Declare victory in your life. If you decree a thing, it will be established.
- Operate in the office of the prophet and call those things that are not as though they were.
- Profess your faith in the true and living God.
- You affirm, meaning you pronounce the outcome of this battle, I am healed, I am free, I am whole, I am healthy, I am wealthy, my children are safe.
- Fight in the Holy Ghost, use your prayer language.
- Put on the whole armor of God
- Be obedient to Christ
- Worship and praise
- Pray

"The effectual fervent prayer of a righteous man availeth much". Meaning this particular type of prayer puts forth power. It is this type of prayer that is directed towards God with great effort. Prayer that is effectual and fervent wields power in the same way that David wielded his slingshot. The power wasn't in the slingshot nor the stones, but in what David decreed with His mouth. This type of prayer is not a blanket type of prayer, but when we pray effectually and fervently, we are making a proclamation in an official definite way. We pray specifically, clearly and precise in relation to a particular person, place, thing, situation.

Most of us are praying, but we must now move on to praying with intent, praying in specifics and then aiming our prayers at a target. When something is done with intent, it is done purposefully, and it has been clearly formulated and has a clear aim.

God hears the prayers of the righteous. *"And this is the confidence that we have in him, that, if we ask any thing according to his will, he heareth us".*

How can we know this? Because we have confessed our sins to a God who is faithful and just to forgive us and cleanse us from all unrighteousness. Not just for the sake of getting answered prayer, but for the sake of His will in our lives and in the earth, *"thy will be done on earth as it is in heaven"*.

When Jesus' disciples said, *"Lord teach us to pray"*, He taught them by saying, *"when you pray say: Our father which art in heaven"*. You must say our father: because He is the creator and originator of everything. *"Which art in heaven"*. You have to let it be known where your prayer is to be going, not to a human father on earth but to the Father who is in heaven. *"Hallowed be thy name"* meaning, I acknowledge your name, I declare that your name is sacred, it is holy, and it is not to be taken in vain or regarded as being worthless.

When you learn how to pray in this manner you can be confident that *"whatsoever you ask, you know that you have the petitions that you desired of him"*.

5. Pain teaches us how to fight giants

When any opposition has come into our lives, we have learned how to go the Lord and expressed our displeasure and anger over it. Even David said, *"I cried unto the LORD with my voice; with my voice unto the LORD did I make my supplication. I poured out my complaint before him; I shewed before him my trouble"*. In going to the Lord in prayer, we learned that the Lord loves us, He has our back, that He is our defense, and our strong tower.

We prayed and God answered, not always in the way that we thought He should, but never the less, His answer was always best for us. And because we knew that the Lord would handle all of our problems, we have had an indirect resistance to opposition and were able to avoid direct confrontation with the enemy.

Just like a child who has been picked on by a bully for the first time, our instinct has always been to run and tell God knowing that He will take care of the situation because He is our daddy. It has been easy to say; I'm going to pray about it as we expressed to God and to others the hostility that we felt. But that hostility was never directed to the offender. We say, even the ark angel didn't rail against the devil but said, *"Satan the Lord rebuke you"*. Therefore, we have thought, what need do I have to fight. God's got this.

But a time always came when a parent would say, if they hit you one more time you better fight back. And we paced the floor trying to figure out how, when and where we were going to fight hoping that we would not need to fight at all. If we were to face our bully, we wanted to make sure that we came home with the victory and not just a black eye. Nevertheless, we fought because we had to.

Our confrontational stance in that situation may not have kept every future bully from bothering us, but we were able to move on with our lives and not be hindered by fear of something that we felt was too big for us to defeat.

You must know that all of yesterday's victories were necessary for your life. With every victory you became stronger, wiser and each fight conditioned your mind for the next and taught you what to do and what not to do. And each victory has prepared you for that giant that you are facing or about to face.

That word giant means gigantic, exceeding the usual or expected (as in size, force, or prominence). Giants are not your everyday common opponent nor are they the things that you have become accustomed to dealing with. But giants show up in your life when you are at the doorway to your next level. They show up as something greater than you have ever had to deal with before. You will see the giant standing in between you and your future, blocking the way to your destiny. You will then have to make a decision, fight or flight.

There are giants that have been assigned to your life; principalities, powers, rulers of darkness of this world, spiritual wickedness in high places. All the giants in your life will be related meaning, they will be connected to each other in some way, but they are not all the same.

There are things that are happening in your life that are related, this situation is connected to that situation. However, we must confront the main giant first. Deal with the one that is standing before you right now, the one that is making all of the noise. He is the one that is between you and your next. Once you take him out, a way will be made for you to get rid of the others, even if the Lord has to send you help to do it.

Note: We cannot accept nor allow giants to stand in our way and stop us without active response or active resistance. *"Resist the devil and he will flee"* the word says. That word "resist" means to oppose or actively resist.

When facing the giants in our lives, we cannot be passive aggressive through simply praying. Giants aren't intimidated by your prayer life; they aren't running just because they see you praise. Giants aren't worried when you study the word, nor do they care how well you preach or teach. The only way to defeat a giant is through confrontational warfare.

Confrontational warfare is a hostile face to face encounter where you face up to and deal with that giant. There will always come a time when you must go into warfare with the intent to kill any giant that opposes the plan of God for your life and your ability to perform the duties that you were anointed to perform. If you have been anointed to a particular assignment, position, duty, or work, you must be willing to say, I'm not playing with this situation but I'm going to stop this giant by killing it and taking its head off (remove its power).

Confrontation is always backed up with intent and it is empowered by strategy. David wasn't conversing with Goliath, he intended to kill him. He purposed and determined that Goliath was going to die and that he was going to be the one to kill him.

There are certain experiences that will come into your life that only you are equipped to handle. There are giants that only you can kill meaning, there are situations that only you can do something about.

Often, we intend to do something about it but because we really don't know how to deal with it, we avoid it and allow it to taunt us, speak against us and the power of our God in our lives. But how badly do we want to shut it up.

Goliath had not killed anyone when David encountered him, nor had he drawn his sword as of yet. But the bible says he was defying the armies of God. That word defy means to jeopardize or to put (someone or something) into a situation in which there is a danger of loss, harm, or failure. That risk alone was worth killing it.

Certain risks are acceptable to take for the sake of progression, however there are somethings that are too risky to keep in our lives. We have to be willing to say; I'm not going to jeopardize this next level opportunity for that. Or I'm not going to jeopardize the call that is on my life because it is too valuable, and it cost me too much pain to get here. So, I must confront this giant and kill it.

Confrontational warfare also demands strategy. You may remember that we talked about strategy in the previous chapter. Uncertainty is a breeding ground for fear. But when you go to the Lord for the strategy which will include using what you already know, what you are already an expert at, you will be fearless in the confrontation. David didn't use Saul's armor, he used what he had successfully used in the past to kill a bear and a lion, which was his slingshot and the power of his confession of what he planned to do to Goliath.

When David ran up on Goliath, he didn't wait or hunker down for the giant to come for him, but it was a preemptive strike. Meaning we must act in order to prevent (an anticipated event) from happening. Somethings we can't wait for, hoping the situation corrects itself, but we must preempt it from happening before it wrecks our future.

David had a choice when it came to confronting Goliath. He really didn't have to do it. He could have brought his brothers their lunch and went back home to tend to his father's sheep. However, when we decide beforehand that we can't defeat a giant or that we don't need to, we forfeit future victories that would lead to new levels in our lives. David went on after that to fight many more battles and won with the help of the Lord. He was known for all of his many victories in battles but none more notable than his first public victory as a seventeen-year-old boy against the giant Goliath that he won with a stone and a sling shot.

Over a decade later after the death of Saul and after David was anointed King over Judah, the bible says. in 2 Samuel 21:15 -22, *"Moreover the Philistines had yet war again with Israel; and David went down, and his servants with him, and fought against the Philistines: and David waxed faint. And Ishbibenob, which was of the sons of the giant, the weight of whose spear weighed three hundred shekels of brass in weight, he being girded with a new sword, thought to have slain David. But Abishai (David's nephew) the son of Zeruiah succoured him, and smote the Philistine, and killed him. Then the men of David sware unto him, saying, Thou shalt go no more out with us to battle, that thou quench not the light of Israel. And it came to pass after this, that there was again a battle with the Philistines at Gob: then Sibbechai (David's guard) the Hushathite slew Saph, which was of the sons of the giant. And there was again a battle in Gob with the Philistines, where Elhanan (David's guard) the son of Jaareoregim, a Bethlehemite, slew the brother of Goliath the Gittite, the staff of whose spear was like a weaver's beam. And there was yet a battle in Gath, where was a man of great stature, that had on every hand six fingers, and on every foot six toes, four and twenty in number; and he also was born to the giant. And when he defied Israel, Jonathan (David's nephew) the son of Shimea the brother of David slew him"*.

In this passage we see four more giants, one of which was Goliath's brother and the others, scholars say, were his sons. Going back in time we also know that David had chosen five smooth stones just to handle Goliath, so we thought. However, I believe that under the unction of the anointing that was poured out on him at age seventeen and in his office of a prophet (one of the five-fold ministry gifts) he knew that there would be four more giants that he would have to face and He believed that the Lord would still give Him that same victory whenever that time came.

When that time arrived David had already fought many battles and had waxed faint, (he was weary) but the men that were assigned to his destiny said, *"Thou shalt go no more out with us to battle, that thou quench not the light of Israel"*, you can't do this, but God can and in God we boast too, just like you did!

Whenever you confront your giants, it gives the people that have been assigned to your life the power to confront giants too. Our refusal to deal with the things that stand in our way to purpose not only hinders our progression, but the progression of everyone and everything that is connected to us. But here is what I love about this, even though David couldn't fight those giants himself, God raised up four men under David's command whom he used to kill the last four giants and the Lord still accounted the victory to David by faith, along with his men. When you win, everyone attached to you wins.

"These four were born to the giant in Gath, and fell by the hand of David, and by the hand of his servants". They no longer terrorized Israel or mocked God as they had in David's youth under Saul.

CHAPTER 4

The Importance of Experiencing Pain

Hebrews 6:1 says, *Therefore leaving the principles of the doctrine of Christ, let us go on unto perfection"*. This passage is saying, "Let us go on from the beginning things, from the things that brought you into salvation and move on to a state of moral and spiritual intelligence and a high mental capacity".

A high mental capacity is:
Your ability to comprehend, to understand and profit from your experiences.

You must begin to see each experience for what it is, know that trouble is not sent to take you out and then mentally seize that opportunity to grow. You must also gain an understanding of what the Lord is trying to say to you and about you through those experiences, and then be willing to do as instructed.

Experiences are simply character tests. Your character is the mental and moral qualities that distinguish you, that make you, you. It is your nature, your personality, your disposition, your temperament, and your mentality all of which must be tested.

Your character is made up of these qualities:

a. How you act every day of the year.
b. How you handle people and situations.
c. How you process your thoughts.
d. How you come to the conclusions that you come to.

Your character is who you really are. One of the hardest things for us to do is to face the truth about who we really are. There is a real difference in who we really are in the eyes of people, who we think we are, and more importantly, who God says that we are.

In your opinion, what would others say about your character?

___

What do you say about your own character?

___

What would the Lord currently say about your character?

___

We have been created in the image or semblance of God, which is His apparent form, even though the reality of who we are outside of Him is vastly different. And, we have been created *"after His likeness"*. We are the representation of God in the earth.

The truth of us is likened unto God and our representation of Him should reflect that as well. However, there are flaws in our character that have been caused by our sin nature which must be corrected through the hardships we are made to experience.

1 Peter 5;10 says, *"But the God of all grace, who hath called us unto his eternal glory by Christ Jesus, after that ye have suffered a while, make you perfect, stablish, strengthen, settle you"*.

That word suffered means: to have a sensible experience. Sensible experiences are the things that effect you and leave you with a sensation or impression.

   a. A sensation is a feeling or perception resulting from something that happened to you: (what they did to you, what they said to you, how they treated you and how it made you feel while you were experiencing it).

   b. An impression is an idea, feeling, or opinion about something or someone, especially one formed without conscious thought. What they did or said has now left me angry, bitter, resentful after the incident has ended.

These sensations and impressions must be dealt with in the process of "character development". Through character development you will not only be tested, but you will also go through a series of changes in your life and you will have to learn how to function in these experiences in a way that is pleasing to God. You must learn how to handle yourself according to the word of God in every situation that comes up in your life without freaking out, without falling apart, without giving up every other day, without acting ungodly or doing anything contrary to the word of God, and come to an understanding of the things in your life that have cause you to be hurt or offended and deal with these things on a daily basis.

Once your character has been developed to match the character of Christ, the Lord will have full control over you knowing that you are now ready to do all of His will.

The Lord told his people, "Awake, awake; put on thy strength, O Zion; put on thy beautiful garments, O Jerusalem, the holy city". Rise up, put on your might and your power and let your majesty, your dignity as well as your character be strong.

One of the definitions of that word awake is renown. Many of you reading this book are going to be renown. You are about to become famous if you are not already. It won't matter if that's not your aspiration, but you will be renown because the Lord needs to use you in places that others cannot get into. Therefore, He is going to make you famous so that He can shine through you while placing you before great men. Soon, people are going to talk about you, (not in the way that they once did), but they are going to speak in awe about who you have become.

However, it won't be because of your education, or how you worked hard for that status, or how you were able to make moves, or how well you branded yourself. It won't be those types of things that will make you renown, it won't even be about what you had to overcome to get there. How you overcame is what is going to make you notable. How you got there is what is going to give you public acclaim and cause people to commend you and talk about how beautiful you are.

The bible says, "Out of Zion, the perfection of beauty, God hath shined". Zion is called the perfection or the completeness of beauty, beauty at its finest. A matured type of beauty, as if it has finally come into its own, beauty that was being groomed and prepared for its final debut, just as Esther was prepped for her moment with the King.

You can tell what effect a situation has had on a person by how they look on the other side of it. The same with you. You will either go through and look as if though it nearly took you out of here, you will go through and look as if though it never happened, or you will go through and look like Moses who had to cover his face because of the glory of God that was all over Him.

That type of glory that came out of Moses, only happens to those that have had to stay in the presence of God in order to rise from something into position. These are the people that had to come up out of something but lost their pride during it, those who got up from something devastating with increased love and compassion for others, or almost came back from the dead, but learned what grace really was through it all. This type of beauty is reserved for those who have risen out of the ashes after losing everything, but during the process they were emptied out of themselves so that the life and ministry of Jesus is now alive in them.

These are the people whom others called an outcast saying, "This is Zion, whom no man seeketh after". Because it looked like you weren't going to come back from that, people stopped caring about you, they stopped calling you, doors that were once opened were shut in your face as people began to walk out of your life, but you learned how to trust in God and Him alone.

Psalms 48:2-3 says, "Beautiful for situation, the joy of the whole earth, is mount Zion, on the sides of the north, the city of the great King". Zion was beautiful because of its position, its height, its elevation. We are impressed by the so-called elevation of a person. However, Zion was not beautiful because of its position or because of its elevation, it was beautiful because of how it got to its position. That phrase *"beautiful for situation"* means "it rises up beautifully". It is beautiful because of how it rises and because it overcame situations with excellency and with outstanding and valuable qualities.

You see, it's not just that you overcame, but people need to know exactly how you overcame. How did you get here? Did you manipulate the situation? Did you do what you wanted to do, did you step over people and mistreat people? Exactly how did you come up to this position"?

We have no problem telling our testimony about why we have a certain status, "I am here because I wanted to help people, because there is a word in me, because God has anointed me to do this". We don't have a problem justifying our position and trying to prove to people why we belong here. But let's tell the truth, exactly how did you get here? Because how you got here, will determine what you do here, and it may even determine if you get to stay here.

If the pain and sufferings in your life have really been successful in establishing you to be who you say that you are, people will know it because you will be stable. We talked about being stable in our chapter on laying a right foundation. But I want to reiterate this point. Many are unstable because what we have gone through has made us emotionally and mentally unbalanced. Especially those of us who did not allow the Lord to really deal with us in it. Most people want the Lord to deal with the situation but won't let him deal with them in it.

Therefore, we are unstable meaning, we can't be held secure in position and because we are unstable, we really can't effectively minister to the people. We really won't care about the people; we will be more concerned about the position than the heart or the needs of those within our sphere of influence.

If you don't let the process do its work in you, you will be so unstable until no one can say anything to you about how crazy you are for fear of getting cussed out, or for fear of you leaving and going somewhere else where somebody will let you be unstable simply because of your gift or your abilities.

In Isaiah 52:2 the Lord told Zion, *"Shake thyself from the dust; arise, and sit down, O Jerusalem: loose thyself from the bands of thy neck, O captive daughter of Zion"*. The Lord is saying to Zion, before you can arise, before you can come on the scene on my behalf and represent me, you have got to shake off the ashes, the debris, the mortar, the ore, shake off the flesh, shake off the world, shake off that human nature, that carnal mind and all of that emotionalism. You must shake off those hard places in your heart that need to be made pliable *and get that yoke off your neck.* What in the world are you bound to and why are you still bound to it and you are "God's person of the hour?"

He said, *"Stand fast therefore in the liberty wherewith Christ hath made us free, and be not entangled again with the yoke of bondage".* Let it be apparent to God that those things have fallen off of you and that you are no longer bound to them. He said, if I am going to elevate you, I need you to do this before you can be established by me, before I give you the power of influence over my people.

You see, position proves nothing because we don't know how you got into position. Sidebar; I am no longer impressed by someone's title or their position especially if you don't even know how to speak to me or anyone else. Something's wrong with you if you are still doing those things and your sphere of influence is massive. Those things should have been handled while you were yet in your growth phase. David's character was tried and dealt with while he was tending his father's sheep, not after he was anointed by Samuel. However, he still had to develop into a king through more trials and testings.

If you have not been first proven or tested in obscurity, in those places and things that seem unimportant, if you have not been tried in insignificance meaning you must be tried when you have the quality of being too small or unimportant to be worth consideration, then you have no right to sit down in a place of authority and influence.

Psalms 84:7 says, *"They go from strength to strength, every one of them in Zion appeareth before God".* In other words, they increased, they grew in virtue, in uprightness and in integrity first. Integrity is the quality of being honest, sound with no incorruptibility. We must be honest in our deportment and have strong moral principles, we need to have sound moral character in order for God to not use us and then burn us up.

Know this, just because God is using you, does not mean you are on your way to heaven or that He is pleased with your character. Remember what I taught on earlier concerning Paul and his preparation process? Paul said, *"But I keep under my body and bring it into subjection (I discipline my own self): lest that by any means, when I have preached to others, I myself should be a castaway".*

The bible says they go from strength to strength. In their coming up they increased in moral character and every one of them in Zion has been inspected by God. They have presented themselves before the Lord in their alone time with the Lord, while in His word, during their private worship experience and by way of fasting and He has looked them over and approved them. It is up to each of us to present ourselves before the Lord and allow the Lord to inspect us before we come up before the people. When something is inspected it is looked at carefully in order to learn more about it, to find problems and then solve those problems.

The bible says, *"Let mount Zion rejoice, let the daughters of Judah be glad, because of thy judgments"*. Rejoice because the LORD has decided that you are right, not because the people have made that determination of you. Be glad because He has deemed you worthy of positioning. He has caused you to be able to stand. Rejoice because the Lord has made a formal decree about you and found you to be suited for His purpose and plan for your life.

Saul was elevated by the people and was unstable in performing the duties to which he was chosen. His character was undeveloped, and his flaws became obvious by the way he handled God's business. However, David was already decided upon by the Lord for His plan and His purpose even before Saul was chosen. The Lord said concerning David, *"I have found David the son of Jesse, a man after mine own heart, which shall fulfil all my will"*.

CHAPTER 5

The Fruit of Your Thoughts

Whenever the Lord calls us to do something, we can be assured that once He started the process in us, He immediately begins to prepare us for the call. After we have been matured and we have completed that time of preparation, the Lord then releases us to walk in it. The bible says, *"He who hath begun a good work in you will perform it until the day of Jesus Christ"*. All we need to do is to have a "let" in our spirit and allow God to do what he needs to do in us.

And yet, many of us get a glimpse of what the Lord is going to do in us, and we immediately expect to be released to do it so that we can prove that we heard the Lord correctly. Some of us need to resist that proving spirit, that spirit that tries to make us jump into a false position just to prove to people that we are "called" or that we are qualified for a particular assignment.

We don't need to prove anything to anybody. *"Whom he called, them he also justified: and whom he justified, them he also glorified. What shall we then say to these things? If God be for us, who can be against us"*? The Lord's plan for our lives isn't contingent upon our strength and abilities, nor on the approval of man, because *"it is not by might nor by power, but by my spirit saith the Lord of host"*.

We are to be led (moved by influence or persuaded) by the Spirit of God the ruwach, the breath, the wind or the Mind of God, and not by people's opinions, our own thoughts or our own knowledge. *"Lean not unto thine own understanding, in all thy ways acknowledge him and he shall direct thy paths."* Meaning, we don't support ourselves, we don't rely on or rest on our own knowledge, or our agenda and our own wants and desires. But we recognize God as being God and we surrender our will over to his leading. *"For as many as are led by the spirit of God* (by the mind of God) *they are the sons of God"*.

We cannot be led by this carnal mind. Jesus asked his disciples, *"What think ye"*? What do you think about this? Eventually what we think is going to begin to produce some kind of fruit, but will that fruit be acceptable to God?

The Lord spoke in the book of Jeremiah the sixth chapter, *"Hear, O earth: behold, I will bring evil upon this people, even the fruit of their thoughts, because they have not hearkened unto my words, nor to my law, but rejected* it". Many have been fooled by the thoughts of men. There are many Christians who thought they were seeing a manifestation of the word of God, however they were simply seeing the fruit of their own thoughts and they believed their own thinking and were led astray. How dangerous. If it doesn't line up with the whole word of God, line upon line precept upon precept, then it isn't God. It is simply someone's thoughts.

"The LORD knoweth the thoughts of man", and He says, *"they are vanity"*. The thoughts of man will only lead us away from the Lord. This is why we are to have no confidence in the flesh, we are not to rely on the flesh, or come into agreement with that which is flesh. *"For they that are after the flesh do mind"* (or set their affections on) *"the things of the flesh; but they that are after the Spirit the things of the Spirit. For to be carnally minded is death; but to be spiritually minded is life and peace. The carnal mind is enmity against God"*. It is hostile towards God, it is hatred towards God and, it is a reason for opposition against God. It is the opposite of everything that He is and we don't want to find ourselves opposing God or in conflict with His will.

When we are led by His Spirit, the Spirit of God will lead you into places where you never dreamed that you would be in. But, if your mind is not renewed you will reject what the Lord wants to do in you because it doesn't feel good to you, or it doesn't look right to you. Your flesh desires to please itself, to make itself happy, and you cannot afford to forfeit the will of God in exchange for a painless life.

This is why Paul said in the book of Romans 13:14, *"But put ye on the Lord Jesus Christ, and make not provision for the flesh, to fulfil the lusts thereof"*. That word provision means forethought or to consider in advance. Jesus had no confidence in the flesh. He didn't trust it, He didn't obey it, He knew exactly what He *was* capable of doing in the flesh, because the bible says He was *"tempted in all points like as we are, yet without sin"*.

He also knew what He was not capable of doing in the flesh because He told his disciples, *"Watch and pray, that ye enter not into temptation: the spirit indeed is willing, but the flesh is weak"*. Our flesh is weak. and it keeps us from:

    a. Maintaining

    b. Being steadfast and unmovable

    c. Having longevity and stick-to-it-ness

    d. Being conquerors

    e. Abstaining from evil

    f. Binding the enemy

g. Being obedient to the word of God and the will of God

We need to understand that the flesh is the devil's playground and operating in the flesh not only breeds rebellion, but it is a precursor or the introduction into deception.

When we are in our flesh, we become vulnerable to the devil's seductive voice. The seducing spirit is the counterfeit spirit of the power of God. It looks like God but has no real power to change lives. It always comes in agreement with our will or with what we want. It is fleshly and emotional, and it makes us "feel" good, thinking we are feeling GOD. It talks like the Spirit of the Lord, but it is wrapped in lies, half-truths and hypocrisies.

The bible says in I Timothy 4:1, *"Now the Spirit speaketh expressly, that in the latter times some shall depart from the faith, giving heed to seducing spirits, and doctrines of devils"*. These seducing spirits come when you are in your flesh and:

a. Trick unstable souls

b. Speak evil of the things that they don't understand

c. Speak great words that profit nothing

d. Entice and entrap through the lusts of the flesh

e. They promise liberty (you will be free from pain and suffering) but they themselves are in bondage to evil. They are without feeling, they care nothing about you (but will deceive you into thinking they do), they simply want you to abort the mission that God has for your life, so that you will forfeit your inheritance in support of their own agenda.

The bible says, *"Let no man deceive you with vain (or empty) words. For because of this cometh the wrath of God upon the children of disobedience. Be ye not partakers with them. For ye were sometimes darkness, but now are ye light, walk as children of light. The fruit of the spirit is in all goodness and righteousness and truth, proving what is acceptable unto the Lord"*. It is the fruit of your thoughts that does the proving, and it is the fruit of the spirit that proves exactly who you are and whose you are and whether you have been called or not. *"A tree is known by the fruit it bears. A good tree brings forth good fruit and a corrupt tree brings forth corrupt fruit"*.

Your fruit is what is produced out of your thought processes.

You can tell when fruit is ripe or mature on a tree because it can be easily plucked from the tree or it will fall to the ground where it can easily be gathered and eaten. The tree with ripe fruit yields or gently gives its fruit away. But un-ripened fruit must be plucked or removed abruptly or forcibly from a tree.

Mature fruit comes from a man that thinks and meditates on God's word. This man *"shall be like a tree planted by the rivers of water, that bringeth forth his fruit in his season; his leaf also shall not wither; and whatsoever he doeth shall prosper"*.

CHAPTER 6

Experiences, Biblically Speaking

Now that we have talked about what the experiences should accomplish in your life, let us look at the ways in which we go through experiences from a biblical standpoint.

Isaiah 43:2 says, " *When thou passest through the waters, I will be with thee, and through the rivers, they shall not overflow thee: when thou walkest through the fire, thou shalt not be burned; neither shall the flame kindle upon thee*".

In this scripture we see three different elements in which one is said to come into contact with or to pass by or through. I have listed them in their order of mention in scripture.

1. Waters

Waters are transitory events that come into our lives. These may be the everyday occurrences that transpire within the life of the believer that we are to quickly overcome and not let these situations affect us, cause us to be moved from our position or stumble in the way.

Transitory events are situations that are meant to be temporary in nature and soon pass away if we refuse to dwell in or on them and keep progressing forward. It is in these types of experiences that we learn how to say, "It's not that serious" and we remain "unbothered" by them and quickly see it and move on.

Water dries quickly without leaving a mark. There are certain situations that touch us directly or indirectly that do not warrant a reaction from us. However, we get hung up on the small things and make them into big things when we should have been unbothered by those things when they first made their appearance in our life.

2. Rivers (or floods).

Rivers in this passage are situations that have the potential to overwhelm you. You will notice throughout this book that we will discuss how to deal with overwhelming situations. However, we will briefly touch on these types of events now.

Rivers are a series of events that come into your life that try to cause you to feel as if you are completely covered and surrounded or they can be one major event that seems too difficult for you to handle. You may feel like these things will overtake you and wash you away, but you must know that the bible says in Isaiah 59:19, *"when the enemy shall come in like a flood, the Spirit of the Lord shall lift up a standard against him"*, shall cause him to disappear.

It is important for you to correctly discern what each situation that comes into your life means by asking yourself, "Are these waters or are these floods (rivers)"? Identification is key to defeating the devil. When you can properly recognize what is happening in your life by knowing where it came from, what purpose it will serve, and how you should handle it according to the category that you will be able to place it in, you will be able to get through it and go through with the peace of God, knowing that these things have no power to touch nor affect you in a harmful way.

Here is a list of situations that may happen in an average person's life. Beside each situation, choose whether you think the situation can be classified as water or floods.

Car breaks down as soon as you get the job that you needed. _____
A friend tells your enemy your deepest secret. _____
You lose your job right after you buy your dream house. _____
Your spouse confesses that he/she is having an affair. _____
Your boss belittles you in front of your co-workers. _____
You break your leg falling down the stairs. _____
You get passed up for a promotion that you deserved._____
You lose your wallet with all your Christmas shopping money in it. _____
You are diagnosed with high blood pressure. _____
You lose your house in a fire. _____
You suddenly must take in and raise your grandchild. _____
Someone cuts you off while driving and scrapes your car. _____
Your best friend stops talking to you after a disagreement. _____
Someone takes a parking space that you waited for._____
Your child gets caught shoplifting._____
Someone tells a lie about you._____

An important statement in this scripture that must not be overlooked says, we will *"pass through"* the waters and the rivers. That phrase "pass through" also means to pass by". When we pass by a thing, that means that the condition or situation is external in nature. We come into close proximity to it, we see it, we experience it but it can happen without affecting us to the point that we must act upon it. In other words, that situation has happened, however it is up to you to make the choice to be "unbothered" by it, or react to it, even though it has no real relevance in your life other than the power that you give it. We can be in a situation and yet not let the situation get in us. We can be in the water or in the river, but if the water or the river gets in us, that water has the potential to kill us.

3. Fire.

Notice, we have passed through the waters and the floods as the scripture has stated however, the bible says that we will "walk" through the fire. There is a vast difference in passing through and in walking through a situation.

That word walk in this scripture means:
    Proceed - to move forward
    Die - to die to self
    Live - to be quickened
    Prosper - to succeed, thrive, flourish.

This fire is defined as a theophany which is the manifested presence of God that encounters you. There are situations in your life that have come into your life so that you can have an encounter with the Lord, one that will be life altering in a way that will thrust you forward. These are situations that will affect you in a major way and have the potential to destroy you, that is, if God is not with you in it.

In my book, "Fire of God, What Do You Do When It All Burns Down", I talk about my encounter with the Lord as I walked through the death of my beloved sister. That fire that came in my life affected me in a way that totally transformed my entire life as I walked through it, lived in it and came out of it with a mind that was yielded to God and a will to perform whatever He desired. It also had the power to kill my purpose, my mission, my destiny and even take my life and would have, had it not been for the Lord who manifested Himself in a very real way in that fire. .

God always and without fail, manifests or makes himself known by way of fire. The bible says in the book of Hebrews, *"our God is a consuming fire"*. That word consume means: to do away with completely. Meaning, when we come into the consuming fire of God, it will do away with:

1. Our old sin nature
2. Our past
3. Our old life
4. Our old way of thinking that keeps us bound
5. Our sicknesses and diseases
6. Our immaturity
7. Our flesh
8. Our will

John the Baptist said. *"I indeed baptize you with water unto repentance: but he that cometh after me is mightier than I, whose shoes I am not worthy to bear: he shall baptize you with the Holy Ghost, and with fire"*.

It takes the fire of God to:

1. Transform us from our miserable unfulfilled lives.
2. Help us to reproduce the works of Jesus.
3. Give us the passion that we need for His word, for His work and for His mission.

Webster defines fire as an "exothermic chemical reaction that emits heat and light". An exothermic chemical reaction means that for fire to exist there must be four things at work:

   1. Fuel: The thing that is consumed to produce energy.

We are the fuel when we become consumed by the fire of God. This old nature, our will, our desires must continually be purged or burned up. We must die to self, humble ourselves and submit ourselves to God. The more of us that gets burned up the more fuel that is produced to do the works of God.

   2. An oxidizing agent: Oxygen.

We must be full of the word of God for it is an oxidizing agent (or oxygen). His word is the air that we breathe, it is the breath of life. If fire is exposed to pure oxygen, combustion accelerates and there will most likely be an explosion. Anytime that logos in us reacts to the rhema word of God, the quickening word, there will be an explosion in us that will consume everything that we encounter!

3. Heat or fervency: Zeal

When something is fervent it is heated to the boiling point. The bible calls this type of heat, zeal. Zeal causes us to be restless, it causes us to lose sleep, to walk the floors, to pray, to get it done. Zeal makes a person not stop until the assignment is done.

4. An uninhibited chemical reaction: Obedience.

There must be an action in us that will keep on reproducing the same action. That action is obedience to the word of God. Obedience is the action that keeps us obedient and it keeps the fire of God burning on the inside of us. Disobedience will kill our zeal and take us out of the presence of the Lord.

The devil doesn't mind if you warm yourself in God's presence. He is not bothered if you simply get close enough to God to be "ok", to be comfortable enough to remain a lukewarm individual with no passion, drive or zeal, just as long as there is no real encounter with the awesome presence of the Lord. He wants to keep you at a distance knowing that if you get close to the fire of God, he will be exposed.

Acts 28:3-6 says, *"And when Paul had gathered a bundle of sticks, and laid them on the fire, there came a viper out of the heat, and fastened on his hand. And when the barbarians saw the venomous beast hang on his hand, they said among themselves, No doubt this man is a murderer, whom, though he hath escaped the sea, yet vengeance suffereth not to live. And he shook off the beast into the fire, and felt no harm. Howbeit they looked when he should have swollen, or fallen down dead suddenly: but after they had looked a great while, and saw no harm come to him, they changed their minds, and said that he was a god".*

Paul and the crew had survived their ship crashing into a reef after sailing for many days through rough weather. The Lord had miraculously saved everyone on board according to his promise to Paul that he sent by way of an angel telling Paul that he could not die on that ship because he would have his opportunity to stand before Caesar and preach the gospel which was Paul's desire. Everyone on the ship was kept alive and made it to the Island of Malta.

It was customary that those who were being kept warm by a fire, help in the gathering of sticks to keep the fire going. Paul also gathered sticks to keep the fire going. However, he unknowingly gathered a snake along with the bundle of sticks.

Snakes will always come out when they are close to the fire because the consuming presence of God will always expose the devil. The bible goes on to say as soon as Paul laid the sticks on the fire, the viper came out of the heat and fastened on to his hand.

Have you wondered why all of a sudden after you got to a new level in Christ, one that you had not walked in before, trouble came in ways that you never thought possible and not only did it come, it came suddenly, unexpectedly and shockingly?

When you were just warming yourself in God's presence, things were not so bad, but once you began to experience the fire of His presence in a way that caused your desires to change to His desires for your life, the devil began to be exposed from hidden places, through people that you never thought would turn on you, conditions, circumstances in which you would not expect him to show up in. And when he jumped out, the attack was vicious.

I was reading about venomous snakes when I was preparing to preach this particular message to my church a few years ago. I learned that a poisonous snake will chew the venom into their victim and once it latches on it is hard to get it off. The longer you let a poisonous snake stay attached to you, the more likely you are to die. Therefore, you have to immediately shake that snake off of you which is what Paul did.

Even though the bite hurts, the bite is rarely the problem. If the venom or the effects of the bite makes its way through your system and you fail to quickly get the help that you need, it will kill you.

However, it will be your survival and the fact that the poison did not affect you in any way, that will prove to all who have been connected to you who you are in Christ. The men were astonished that Paul did not die. People will be astonished that you survived, but your survival will be contingent upon how much of you has surrendered to God way before that type of trial finds its way into your life.

CHAPTER 7

Types Of Pain

Just as there are many different experiences that we must encounter, there are divers' types of pain that we will experience in this life each with its own purpose and effect.

Let's look at the list that I compiled of some of the major types of pain and sufferings that have been sanctioned by the Lord for us to experience.

1. AGONY: A struggle for victory.
                     Severe mental struggle to do what is right.
                     The final stages of difficulties after prolonged pain.

Agony is one of the most productive types of pain that one could experience. And yet, few will be called to go through it, however if you have been called into this type of pain, it is because you have been divinely selected to suffer in this way. Those that have been brought to the point of agony will not suffer this for their own sakes, but for the sake of others. Meaning the call that is on your life is one that will set the masses free and not just a few. It will be your struggle against your own will to do what is right that will release you to walk in such a calling to the nations.

This type of suffering is only found once in the bible in Luke 22:44 when it says, *"Jesus in the garden was in agony when He prayed"*. The bible says that He prayed to the point that great drops of blood were coming from his pores. The bible also says in 2 Timothy 2:3, *"For consider him that endured such contradiction of sinners against himself, lest ye be wearied and faint in your minds. Ye have not resisted unto blood, striving against sin"*.

That word contradiction means opposition. None of us have opposed our own will to the point of blood shed fighting to bring our will into alignment with the will of God. We will never have to suffer in agony to this extreme since Jesus already gained the victory for us over the will of the flesh when He conquered the flesh in the garden of Gethsemane.

Even though Jesus said, greater works will you do, because I go to the Father, His ministry was to the world in that He was given for the salvation of the entire world, past present and future. None will ever be called to fulfill that mission; it was completed in Christ. However, some will be called to the world in a different manner and those who are, must understand that the cost to walk in this type of calling will be high.

Therefore, few are chosen for this type of assignment and only those whom the Lord has predetermined to do so will walk through the pain of agony.

2. SORROW: Deep distress caused by a loss of something of worth or value
            Disappointments (loss of hope of expectations).

The bible talks about Lot's wife who turned in to a pillar of salt when she looked back on Sodom and Gomorrah as it burned to the ground. I don't believe that she looked back in some sort of longing of a sinful lifestyle that she was taken out of but, because of a loss of hope and believing there was nothing better for her than what she had lost. As bad as her situation was, it was her life and the only life that she knew.

If we don't think that there is anything better for us, we will seek out new opportunities to redo what the Lord is bringing us out of. We must understand that if the Lord allows something that seems to be life-altering to come into our lives that brings us to a place of sorrow, it is only because there is a greater good or purpose. Therefore, the Lord does not want us to be sorrowful over what He has permitted to be removed from our life.

The only sorrow that the Lord wants us to have is Godly sorrow, which works repentance. God expects us to be sorry for the sins that we have committed in disobeying His word and His will for our lives. And yet we are sorrier for the things that we lose or the things that are taken away from us than we are sorry for the things that we do to the Lord.

If you take a good hard look at your life, you will see that none of the things that you lost or the things that disappointed you really had the power to hinder you and keep you from being all that you could be in the Lord. As a matter of fact, the loss brought necessary change into your life.

Always remember that everyone suffers with disappointment and sorrow at some point in their lives. The bible is actually full of people with regrets.

Adam and Eve surely must have regretted eating the fruit from the tree.

Sarah regretted giving her handmaiden Hagar to her husband Abraham so that they could give birth to the promised child.

Isaac regretted tricking Esau out of his birthright and stealing the blessing of their father from him.

David regretted killing Uriah in order to cover his sin with Bathsheba.

We may be sorry or regret what happened, but regret does not change the outcome of our actions. However, the Lord gives us grace to live with the fruit of our doings.

You must also understand that there are people and things that were done with you even though you may feel that you were not done with that thing or that person. There were:

- people that were done needing you, you fulfilled your purpose in their life.
- places that you were in for a purpose to supply a need and the need was supplied.
- seasons in your life that came to an abrupt end but, because you do not particularly like how it ended, you believe that you must have "closure" when the only closure that you may get is to move forward.

Make of list of some things have happened in your life that have caused you to be disappointed:

_____
_____
_____
_____
_____
_____
_____
_____
_____
_____
_____
_____
_____

Now make a list of the good things that have happened as a result of those same things that disappointed you:

_____
_____
_____
_____
_____
_____
_____
_____
_____
_____
_____
_____
_____
_____
_____
_____

3. **WRITHING:** Twisting, squirming, tossing.
   Prolonged intense pain.
   A response to great emotional and physical discomfort.

This type of pain comes with travail, which is bearing, bringing forth. We will talk at length about this type of pain in the chapter "Stages of Labor".

4. **ANGUISH:** Heartache.
   Things that hurt the heart or take the breath away.
   Stress - Narrowness, Cramped
   Distress - Anxiety, Difficulties
(From tension due to being focused on one's self or one's own problems).

If not checked, this type of pain can lead to depression which can be unresponsive to help and support.

Take a minute to identify things that you have had to go through that caused you heartache:

_____
_____
_____
_____

_____
_____
_____
_____
_____
_____
_____
_____

How many of those things on your list are you currently focused on?

1.___
2.___
3.___
4.___
More than 4___

Find one item from the previous list and choose to release it from this moment on. List that item below and write out your pledge and your commitment to release it. Then write your prayer to the Lord to help you to let it go.

_____
_____
_____
_____
_____
_____
_____
_____
_____
_____
_____
_____
_____
_____
_____
_____
_____
_____
_____

If you continue to struggle with that one item, return regularly to this page and rehearse your words in your own ears as you recommit to releasing it until it is done. When you have been made aware that the item that you have committed to release from your life is now gone, return to your list and repeat the same process until all the items on your list are no longer relevant in your life.

If you have a continued feeling of anxiety and depression, do not hesitate to seek professional counseling. If you are struggling with thoughts of suicide call the National Suicide Prevention Lifeline immediately at 1-800-273-8255. This number is available 24 hours every day.

5. GRIEF: Deep sorrow.
                      Personal loss that affects your life.
                      Expression of mourning. (Annoyances, Irritations)

(From tension due to being focused on a thing or person). Grief does not affect one's self image, but it can lead to a feeling of hopelessness believing that what one has lost is so irreplaceable that it can't be lived without.

If properly dealt with grief is not constant in its intensity and the sting of the loss diminishes over time with help and support. This does not mean that you will not feel a sense of loss over time, but you will be able to function in it and use that pain for purpose.

There are 5 known stages of grief and loss. They are:

1. Denial

Denial causes us not to feel the full effects of the loss and it keeps us from dealing with the facts. We must know that there are the facts and then there is the truth. The only truth is the word of God no matter what the facts may be. Getting the facts allows us to be able to deal with the facts according to the word of God. Denying the existence of the facts does not change the facts.

2. Anger

Anger is a strong feeling of being annoyed, displeased or hostile towards the one that we believe is responsible for our loss. Many will become angry at God because He is God and we believe that He is the one who is responsible for taking something from us. The bible does say that *"the Lord giveth and the Lord taketh away and His name is to be blessed"*. However, the Lord never allows anything to be removed from our life without a plan for restoration.

The bible lets us know that we can be angry, however we are not to sin in that anger nor let the sun go down upon our wrath. Properly directed anger can move us to purpose, however misdirected or intense anger will drive us to sin.

3. Bargaining.

Here we begin to "make a deal with God". If you do that, I will do this, and we refuse to budge in trying to make the Lord "change His mind" or hold up to what we believe that He should be doing according to His word. But the truth of God's word stands sure and He will not be bargained with. However, if the Lord does do what you asked him to do in the way that you bargained for, you can rest assured that He will call in your end of the bargain and you may not like what transpires in your life to cause you to hold up to what you said.

4. Depression

As we stated earlier depression comes from being anxious about a situation. When we become depressed it is because our focus is on a thing and not on what the Lord has said. There is no exclusive answer to how to handle depression.

Depression is often "tip toed" around in the house of God. If it is tackled it is often dealt with as demonic influence or possession. Because the church does not know how to handle depression, we force people to "get over it" or tell them that they need to pray more or study their word more making them feel even more hopeless especially if they are trying but still struggling with depression.

Depression cannot be treated with one counseling session. Some forms of depression are chemically induced by an imbalance in the body or the depression may be situational or even seasonal. It may be difficult to diagnose the type of depression a person is experiencing and get to the root of the depression without extensive therapy and possibly long-term counseling.

I truly believe that the church needs counselors and professionals within the body to partner with the leadership staff in helping people to overcome depression.

5. Acceptance

It is so important that we learn how to accept the will of God for our lives. We must receive it with approval or favor and not consider what God has done as unjust treatment. To accept also means:

- to undertake the responsibility, duties, honors, etc., of: (Do what I have you to do, to come out of it, learn the lessons, behave appropriately in it)
- to accommodate or reconcile oneself to
- to regard as true or sound; believe
- to receive as to meaning; understand
- to acknowledge
- to accept as a gift

What we refuse to accept, we will begin to loathe just as the Children of Israel did when they became tired of eating manna.

We then begin to show our disapproval of what the Lord has allowed to happen by complaining aloud. And even if we aren't complaining, we are murmuring which is silently complaining about something. And by murmuring we show ourselves to be stubborn against God, or to have a hostile mind towards Him which is a mind that rejects what God is doing or what He has said.

Well how are we rejecting the trial that has come into our lives? By not agreeing with it. If we come into agreement with all of it by saying "nevertheless not my will but your will be done", we can make ourselves firm and strong so that we can prevail over whatever it is that is causing us to think we have a right to be discontent. When we are not content, we show that we have no respect towards God or His word in our lives.

> David said in Psalms 142:2, "*I poured out my complaint before him; I shewed before him my trouble*". But David wasn't talking about the type of complaining that we often do. He was saying, "I communicated my troubles to the Lord and to Him alone in prayer. I had a conversation with Him about my life and all my issues, because "*He is my refuge and my*

portion in the land of the living". He is my lot in this life and in Him I have everything that I need, that I want, and I have it all in abundance. He is my situation; He is my condition and He is my circumstance". Because I agree with his word, I shall not suffer lack, I shall not fail, whatever I do, I will prosper in it, I shall not be made lower than who He has said in His word that I am, and I won't be destitute or empty.

One of the hardest things for us to do is to learn how to accept the will of God when it pertains to something that means everything to us. When my sister was diagnosed with stage four cancer, we refused to believe anything more than the word of God concerning her healing, but never ever talked about even the remote possibility of death. In doing so, we often fail to prepare ourselves to handle the death of our loved ones and we also fail to help that person to prepare for their own ending of life.

Even though I knew that my sister was ready for the afterlife, those of us who would be left behind once she passed away, were not prepared to live life without her. Once she passed away, insurance papers had to be found to prepare for her funeral. Other documents needed to finalize some of her business dealings were hard to find because we were afraid to talk about those things as if though are discussion of what to do if she died, would have somehow negated our faith.

We must begin to understand that there is a natural part of life that includes death. People die. Being an ostrich will not change the fact that our loved ones will eventually die. But dealing with it by first accepting it before it happens, will help them to prepare their own hearts by making peace with God and with those that they may need to make peace with. It will also help us to prepare our own selves to begin the process of life without our loved one. In my book, "Fire of God", I talk extensively about how I had to deal with my sister's diagnosis, her death and learning how to live a full life without her. I encourage anyone who is walking through any hardship in life that seems insurmountable to read that book.

6. ADVERSITIES: Continued difficulties that don't let up.
   Trouble, tightness, being squeezed.
   Boxed in with nowhere to go.

Paul said, *"we are troubled on every side"*. We are compressed from every side, home, job, church, kids and we are being pressed into a smaller space. You may even feel closed in like you are being suffocated. This is because the enemy wants to intimidate you, to restrict you and create a barrier around you in order to make you smaller than what you truly are. David was anointed King over all of Israel, but the enemy wanted to restrict him and keep him in a tight space.

If you are restricted in movement, you will be ineffective in your everyday life. Therefore, in order to break you out of your restrictions, you will need a breakthrough.

A breakthrough is not the same as an open door. The Lord does open doors for us that can be clearly seen, that is if we are looking with our spiritual eyes. Whenever the Lord opens a door, we don't have to kick it open by force. We can easily walk through it because it is a clear and unrestricted pathway to whatever it is that the Lord wants to bring you into.

However, there are times in your life when there is no opened door. You are so surrounded until you see no way out, no way through or around it. It is at these times that the opening must be made by way of force, by breaking through.

Breakthrough isn't about opportunity; it isn't about a chance or a change in your condition or a change in your circumstance. Breakthrough is about forcefully confronting the enemy and breaking through his barriers and going past him in order to defeat him.

If you want breakthrough you will have to force your way, you will have to force yourself to do what you may not want to do. You may need to force yourself to make certain changes in your life, or even force the hand of those that are binding you or restricting your progression in life.

However, you will have to go to the Lord for the "how to" strategy for a successful breakthrough. The bible says, "And David *enquired of God*, saying, *"Shall I go up against the Philistines? and wilt thou deliver them into mine hand?"*, because you can't have breakthrough without instruction.

People who enquire of God, prosper, people who seek God get answers to their problems. God told Joshua, *"Only the LORD give thee wisdom and understanding, and give thee charge concerning Israel"*. Only let God tell you what to do and how to do it. *"Then shalt thou prosper"*.

David understood this principle and said, *"I will enquire within thy temple"*. I will seek, I will look for and I will consider God in the matter. Most of us will never get a breakthrough because we won't go to the Lord in the matter.

Another definition of breakthrough is a sudden advance in knowledge or technique. What you need in order to breakthrough is a different level of information. What you know now isn't going to get you a breakthrough. Therefore, you need to know something different, something that you don't already know. information that is not right in front of your face.

You need a level of information that can only come through intimacy with God. The Lord will only speak to you according to your level of understanding of Him. There are secrets that He reveals to those who have a familiarity with him or those who are in close companionship with Him. Therefore, your breakthrough out of these particular types of pain, will come by way of drawing closer to the Lord in order to receive hidden instructions.

However, the devil will return to test your deliverance and try to pressure you and bind you up again. But if you know the secrets to deliverance you can defeat him on every side.

.

CHAPTER 8

Stages of Labor

God told Jeremiah in 1:5, *"Before I formed thee in the belly, I knew thee and before thou camest forth out of the womb, I sanctified thee and ordained thee a prophet unto the nations"*. The Lord told Jeremiah, I formed you in the womb meaning, I assigned you, appointed you, designated you, I counted you.

You count. You matter because the Lord made you matter when He put you in the womb. It was in the womb that you were included in His plans. You were not insignificant then and you are not insignificant now.

In the womb you were prepared, set apart, honored, made holy and dedicated to a cause. A cause is a reason for an action. You are the reason for a particular situation and action that will happen in the earth. The Lord allowed those things to happen because He had already assigned you:
- to fill it
- to handle it
- to subdue it
- to conquer it
- to walk in it
- to take it
- to live by it

You were not made for things, but things were made for you.

Everything you need for life was given to you in the womb, lungs to breathe, brain to think, mouth to talk, ears to hear, arms to extend, legs to walk, stomach to receive nourishment, your purpose, your destiny, the ability to be what you were designed to be comes by way of the womb. And when your purpose is birthed out of you, it will come forth already equipped to do what it was intended to do.

That womb was the environment that the Lord used to squeeze your life into shape and mold it into form. It is the environment in which the Lord configured your call and fit you for a designated task. But in order to fit you for your call you must go through the difficult process of being brought forth or birthed into purpose. This process happens in stages.

Since you may not realize that the process has begun until you are in the thick of it, there will be no way of aborting the process until it has delivered what the Lord started in the womb. However, if you do not understand what is happening to you once the process has begun, you risk not being able to survive it.

The same as in the natural the bringing forth process is sequential. We will be discussing each one listed below in this chapter.

- Early labor (the onset)
- Active Labor (travail)
- Pushing (bringing forth)

EARLY LABOR

This stage in the process is the onset of hardships and trials that produce painful experiences in our lives. That word onset means:

- Attack
- Assault
- Commence
- Formed

There is a moment, a time, when an attack has been officially launched. It could be an event or a series of events that are connected in some way that will signal to us that the onset or the launch of our birth process has begun.

Isaiah 54:17 says, "*No weapon that is formed against thee shall prosper*". That word weapon means a tool or utensil that is used for a specific purpose. The enemy has designed a tool that he has predetermined to be the right tool to use to put his plan into effect in your life.

It is an untruth that the devil knows everything about you. He does not. He is not God. He does not know what you are thinking, nor what God's plan is for your life. The only information that he knows about you is what is given to him by the Lord and even by you, unknowingly. Therefore, he is constantly watching you, studying you, observing your behavior and how you respond to the different circumstances and conditions that come into your life.

He will form a weapon that is tailored for who you are based on:
- your prior responses
- your inability to overcome certain situations
- the things that you say in the time of trouble
- your everyday reactions
- how you have dealt with the things that have happened to you throughout your life.

The attacks that have come into your life have been predetermined by the enemy for your demise and those same attacks have been predetermined by the Lord for your good. The devil has an intention or an objective for your life, but so does the Lord who permits the enemy's tools to be formed because He knows that they will work for His own objective.

ACTIVE LABOR (Travail)

Travail is not just prayer, and it is not something that you decide to do on your own. We cannot simply say; I am going into travail about this or that situation in my life. Travail is brought upon you. Just as in the natural, we cannot make the labor process progress simply because we want it to. It begins at the time appointed for the baby to come into the world and progression through stages, with each stage requiring a particular amount of time and purpose.

The Lord told Zion, *"Shall I bring to the birth and not cause it to bring forth? Shall I cause to bring forth and shut the womb"?* Not so, since I put something in your womb for you to birth out, I am going to cause you to go into travail to birth it out.

The Lord must allow situations to come into your life because there is no better way to cause you to go into travail than to allow the enemy to afflict you in a way that will threaten the thing that He has put in you to birth out.

As soon as the enemy afflicts that thing that we have invested our heart and our life into waiting for it to manifest, we will stay up all night pacing the floor, praying, crying out to God and pulling out every bit of spiritual arsenal that we have access to because of the intensity of the struggle.

Travail is intense pain that brings on intercession in the Holy Spirit in order to open up a way for what the Lord has placed in you to be birthed out. This is the hardest and often the longest part of the process and it is experienced differently in the life of every one that must go through it. Someone may be able to coach you through it but, they can't tell you exactly what the experience will be like for you. They can only tell you what they have been taught either through study or personal experience. If you listen to a group of women sharing their stories of the birthing process, each will have a very different story to tell, but the outcome will be the same, a baby was born. Therefore, you must be sensitive to the leading and the voice of the Spirit of God to guide you through this phase.

Each person that travails will experience pain in different areas and in different levels of intensity. Some may have higher pain tolerances than others, therefore one may struggle through the process while another will endure what would have taken you out.

Those who are brought into travail will experience the pain in different regions of their lives, just as one laboring woman may feel the pain in her lower back and another may say that she felt it in her abdominal region. In spiritual travail, your home, church, job, physical, mental, emotional or other regions may feel the intensity of the pain causing you to pinpoint your prayer to that region that is experiencing the greatest pain.

Travail is also one of the best ways to bring you into humility and submission because it takes away all your pride! Many women can testify to the fact that when the hardest labor was in process, they did not care what they looked like nor who had access to seeing their most private parts, nor how loudly they screamed and cried out, all that they cared about at that time was surviving the pain.

The closer you come to bringing forth, the more intense travailing becomes for everyone who experiences this stage of the process. When you are close to bringing forth you will experience some of the greatest attacks of your life and those attacks will come in succession or you may have one prolonged experience that may be severe in its effects on your life.

And yet, there are dangers in this phase of the process that may have a detrimental effect on the birthing out of God's promise.

Some difficulties in travail include:
1. Failure to progress:

There is a term when one is running a marathon race called "hitting the wall". The wall is the point where your body and mind are simultaneously tested. It's the perfect intersection of fatigue and diminished mental faculties. It's the exact point where all a runner's pre-race plans go out the window because they have gotten tired. Being tired is a dangerous place to be in, this is why getting proper rest, both spiritually and naturally is so vital.

It will take a vast about of energy and endurance to push the baby out and no one can do it for you meaning, this is the race that is set before you and you alone. Hebrews 12:1 says, *"Wherefore seeing we also are compassed about with so great a cloud of witnesses, let us lay aside every weight, and the sin which doth so easily beset us, and let us run with patience the race that is set before us"*, the one that you have been appointed or destined to run, the race that is present or in front of you.

This race isn't about speed or agility, it's about getting to the end. One of the greatest obstacles in a marathon type of race is hitting that wall, because your mind is at its weakest just when you hit the wall, the place where you need your mind to be the strongest. But Paul said it is at this point that you must "lay aside every weight, and the sin which doth so easily beset you". That word lay aside means to put off or put away the thing which anyone gives up, renounces: when you renounce a thing, you refuse to recognize or abide by that thing any longer. Renounce also means to:

1. Formally declare one's abandonment of a claim, right, or possession. I will open my mouth and speak of what belongs to me according to the word of God and refuse to take possession of what does not belong to me.

2. Declare that one will no longer engage in or support. I wash my hands of my past hurts, my present unfavorable conditions and my fears of the unknown, the things I can do nothing about.

These weights and sins *beset* me meaning;
- they skillfully surround me in order to prevent something from happening
- they slow down my pace
- they come at me in every direction

Therefore, I must lay aside every weight which is:
- whatever is prominent.
- whatever can be easily seen and noticeable.

The weight is stealing my focus and my ability to concentrate and now it has become a burden, pressure and, an encumbrance.

I must also cast it off along with the sin. Sin is:
- missing the mark.
- wandering from the path of uprightness and honor. We can't allow sin in our life to take us off course. We can't keep sinning and expect to be able to keep on moving in the right direction.

In order to overcome these things, it will take willpower and mental reframing. Willpower is the motivation to exercise the will. A person with strong willpower will make decisions even in the face of strong opposition or other contradictory factors. A person with little willpower will give in easily.

To increase your willpower. you must:
- talk to yourself and make yourself keep pressing forward
- encourage and motivate your own self
- stay focused
- ignore the distractions no matter how big the distraction may seem

2. Not enough oxygen to the thing being birthed out:

You may get some indication that will make you think that what you are carrying is in distress, meaning it may look like the promise will die between labor and birth. Things will begin to look like they are falling apart all around you causing it to appear as if what God has spoken will be impossible to perform. If this happens, you must breathe and pull on the word of God which is the oxygen for life. Breathe and concentrate on the word of God, meditate on it day and night until it is birthing time.

3. Baby not positioned right:

You may know what God has said concerning what He has planted in you, but there will be things that may come to set the promise on a different course other than exactly how the Lord has spoken it. God will do exactly what He said He will do. He may not do it the way that we want Him to do it, but He will do it.

Because your mind cannot fathom the greatness of what God has planned to do, you must be willing to make the decision to not do the thing that seems like the promise, but it is not exactly what God said that He would do. If you get another offer other than what the Lord has promised and yet it is the easy way out, meaning, it won't cost you much, you cannot walk in that direction.

Our flesh will always want to find the easy way to obtain the thing of God. However, the easy way will lead you away from the perfect will of God even though it may look like a good offer.

4. Baby's head is too large to enter the canal:

This means that the promise is greater than you expected. Remember, the Lord will always *"do exceeding abundantly above all that you ask or think"*! You may not sense that what the Lord is about to birth out of you is greater than you thought until you are at the end of your time of travail. But when you sense that this promise is massive you will need to receive the help of midwives, those who can pray with you and help you to push the promise out.

The midwives must be ones that you can trust with your life and with the promise that God has placed in you. It may be hard to receive help after you have been betrayed or kicked to the curb by people that you trusted, but you must be willing to trust again and remember this is not all about you, it is about the plan of God being birthed into the earth.

The Lord said in the book of Jeremiah the 9th chapter, *"Consider ye and call for the mourning women, that they may come and send for the cunning women that they may come and let them make haste and take up a wailing. That our eyes may run down with tears and our eye lids gush out with waters. For the voice of wailing is heard out of Zion".*

Those wailing women in scripture were hired professionals who were cunning and skillful at wailing and mourning. They knew how to use words and were skillful in choosing words that would invoke the response they wanted. They knew how to use their own anguish their own grief, their own sorrows, their own burdens to provoke the emotions in others to do the same.

God said, in Isaiah 43:4, *"Since thou wast precious in my sight, thou hast been honourable and I have loved thee, therefore, will I give men for thee and people for thy life"*. Because you will need help to bring forth my plan, I have already assigned people to be with you and to help you to get to your purpose. God sent men to David while he was in the cave, men who fought with him and allowed themselves to submit to him and eventually crowned him king of all of Israel.

Note: You cannot trust everybody, but you will have to trust somebody.

BIRTHING OR BRINGING FORTH

This is the most exciting time in the bringing forth process. You may feel the excitement of new possibilities for your life and the joy of receiving what you have been waiting years for. This is the culmination of years of suffering and you are about to see everything manifested.

As in the natural labor process, when it is time, you will begin to feel pressure along with an urge to push. The pressure will be a continuous force exerted upon your heart to act. Job said in the 32nd chapter and the 18th verse, *"For I am full of matter, the spirit with in me constraineth me"*. What he was saying was, "the spirit of God that is within my heart presses me to the point of bursting". The spirit of God by His grace will influence our hearts in a way that cannot be resisted and then empower us to do that thing that we could not do on our own.

An urge is a strong desire or impulse to do something. However, in the kingdom of God, the Lord does not operate in our impulses, but with our desires which will by this time have come into agreement with His desires for our life. Remember that the thing that we are birthing out is His, it is not ours.

The urge that you feel will be necessary to push or force the process along with power and vigor and it will drive you to complete the process.

It will take power to push this baby out, but it will not be your power, but the power of God so that you can take no credit for what the Lord has done.

We use the term PUSH, "pray, until, something, happens" as a motivation to pray it out. However, the birthing or bringing forth happens only after the travail or the praying period has caused the process to come to maturity. This is not the time to pray, but it is a time for action. This action will be difficult in nature, but your previous prayers will cause you to walk in the power of God and not in your own abilities to bring it to pass.

When it is time to bring forth you will begin to experience extreme discomfort in your life. The discomfort will be so great until you will feel like you must do something in order to manifest the promise. But you must be careful to take no action without the leading of the Spirit of God. You cannot push just because you feel the pressure to push meaning, you cannot be swayed by your emotions. But you must only take action when you have been instructed by God to do so.

There will be a sense of intensity or a force that will drive your life in a direction that you may not be willing to go in, but you will know without a doubt that it is necessary to go that particular way in order to birth the promise out.

Your response at this point in the process is the only thing that will matter. As the events and circumstances in this process begin to unfold through the power of God, you must:

1. Position yourself:

Your posture towards God at this point must be that of "not my will, but thine be done". Your feelings and emotions can have no interaction in the matter as they could endanger the outcome of the process. Because this is the will of God for your life, He will cause everything to have lined up so that He can drive you to the place that He has already prepared for you.

2. Conserve your energy:

Don't fight people nor defend yourself to those who will begin to speak against you. For this battle is not yours, it is the Lord's. There may be people in your life who will not be excited about the new thing that the Lord wants to do in your life, These people will fight you tooth and nail, but you cannot waste the energy that you will need in order to begin this new journey on people who want to hinder it or can't and won't help you anyway. They will talk about you, lie on you and do their best to turn others against you just as the enemies of Jesus did to him, a strategy that ushered Him to the cross.

3. Let Go and Let God:

Yes, this is the most used cliché phrase in all "kingdomness". But in this case, it is the most appropriate. You can do nothing about this process once it has begun, you are not getting out of it, no matter how hard you scream, you must go through it. Therefore, it is best to make your spirit rest in what God is doing and more so in how He is doing it.

Screaming will not help, in that it causes one to tense up. Tensing up will only make the process more difficult. *"Let the peace of God which passes all understanding keep your heart and your mind through Christ Jesus"*. If you feel the urge to scream, let only the praises of God come out of your mouth.

Before you know it, you will see the manifestation of what God has spoken to you with your own eyes. And it will be even more glorious than you imagined that it would be.

CHAPTER 9

Growth, Development and The Wilderness

Earlier we talked about laying a foundation for your life. It is imperative that you are firmly rooted and grounded and planted in the word of God before you attempt to walk in the things that you have been purposed to do. The problem for many is their failure to be planted somewhere so that they can die to their own will and begin to come alive in Christ.

The bible says in John 12:24, *"Except a corn of wheat fall into the ground and die it abideth alone, but if it die it bringeth forth much fruit"*. You must be willing to die to self-exaltation, self-will, selfishness and that "I" mentality and allow the Lord to be seen in and through your life. Therefore, the Apostle Paul said, *"I am crucified with Christ nevertheless, I live. Yet not I, but Christ which liveth in me. And the life which I now live in the flesh* (this new life), *I live by the faith of the Son of God who loved me and gave himself for me"*.

One of the first principles that we must embrace in our lives on this journey of growth and development is submission. For you to learn submission you must begin by learning how to submit to those that the Lord will place over your life to water the seed that the Lord has planted in you in preparation for your destiny. This includes God's authority and the authority that He gave to man by way of the five-fold gifts to the church.

There are many who may say, "I can serve God at home, I can pray and watch church on television, and I don't need to be in a church to do what I have been called to do". This may be true, however, there is a level of obedience that God the Father is expecting us to have in our lives and that first level comes with establishing order in your life.

Psalms 68:18 says, *"Though hast ascended on high, thou has led captivity captive, thou hast received gifts for men, yea for the rebellious also, that the Lord God might dwell among them"*. God has given us apostles, prophets, evangelists, pastors and teachers, not only for the work of the ministry and for the edifying of the body of Christ, but also for the rebel, the stubborn and rebellious one who refuses order, who fails at submission and those who continue to resist the leading of God in the way in which He chooses to lead.

GROWTH

Our walk to maturity begins at the growth stage. We start off as spiritual infants at the new birth phase but quickly progress in our growth. We are to continually be growing in grace and in knowledge by drinking the milk of the word and then we grow to the meat of the word by not just reading and hearing the word of God, but we give ourselves over to studying the word of God for ourselves with deeper revelation and illumination coming from the Holy Spirit.

The bible tells us in 2 Timothy 2:15, *"Study to show thyself approved unto God a workman that neededth not be ashamed, rightly dividing the word of truth"*. Studying is not simply reading a daily scripture or going through the bible in a year. But study in this scripture means that we give diligence to:

- Study the word of God.
- Obey the word of God.
- Submit to the word of God.
- Teach the word of God.
- Live by the word of God.

When we follow this pattern in applying the word of God to our lives, we become accepted and pleasing to God as a laborer and a teacher having no cause to be ashamed. We cannot move in the things of the Lord without being prepared by His word.

Along with our study of His word, our experiences are a part of the growth and preparation process as well. However, each experience must be partnered with the word of God to mature us and strengthen us for His use.

When we allow the growth process to work in us, we will become equipped to:

- Handle the word of God
- Teach the truth correctly
- Teach the truth directly
- Dissect or expound the word of God correctly

We must be able to use the word of God similarly to using a correct tool for a specific purpose. When Jesus was tested in the wilderness by the devil, He was able to use the correct response to each test in order to gain the victory over the snare of the devil. He did not direct the word to the devil as we suppose, but He directed that word at His own flesh to bring it under subjection to the will of God.

It is also important that we learn how to properly teach the word so that those who are under our influence will also grow and mature in their own work. Many people's lives have been altered because of incorrect teaching. We must know the great responsibility that has been place on us to teach the truth and to be able to pinpoint that word where it needs to go. We don't shoot an arrow without aim, nor can we cure a condition without proper treatment. Therefore, the word must be properly aimed to be an effective weapon.

There will come a time when we must be able to "go deep" in our revelations coming from the word of God and our explanation of the word of God to those who will require more than a scripture. We must have an answer for anyone including the wise and the prudent who may be asking questions concerning the plan of salvation and its importance in our lives.

Not only must we go deeper for others, we cannot stay in the shallow end of our salvation and expect to have good success. *"Deep calleth unto deep"*. The Lord is expecting our minds to grow higher and go deeper and wider. Growth is all about expansion!

It took the children of Israel four hundred plus years to grow into a nation. When they first came to Egypt when Joseph was the governor over all of Egypt, Jacob (Joseph's father) and his brothers along with their families, arrived as a small group. It was because of a famine that they went to Egypt and found food and refuge there through the brother that they had once rejected. However, over the next 450 years, they grew to a million strong and became a great nation while still in Egypt their place of growth.

The place of growth is the place:

1. Where you become greater than what you were.
2. Where you enlarge in your strength.
3. Where you learn by doing.

4. Where you grow in value.
5. Where you learn submission and obedience.
6. Where your heart changes.
7. Where you learn to hear God's voice.
8. Where you learn faithfulness.
9. Where you die to self.

Even Jesus *"increased in wisdom and stature and in favor with God and with man"* as stated in Luke 2:52. In other words, He himself had to grow in the natural as well as mature in wisdom, stature and favor. Let's go a little deeper and talk in detail about this.

That word increased means to:

1. Advance - to move forward in a purposeful way.
2. Make Progress - onward in space and time toward a destination.
3. Promote Forward - to be raised to a higher position or rank.
4. Drive Forward - to propel along by force in a specified direction.
5. Profit - gain more than one began with.
6. Wax - to magnify, to become great or important.

Not only must we increase, as Jesus did but we must increase in:

Wisdom - Knowledge of very diverse matters
Skill in the management of affairs
Proper prudence in interactions with men who are not disciples
Skill and discretion in imparting Christian truth

Daniel said, *"He giveth wisdom unto the wise and knowledge to them that know understanding"*. You might ask, well what is knowledge? Knowledge is not simply knowing the word of God because demons know the word of God, sinners know the word of God, the reprobate person knows the word of God.

But knowledge is:

- Cunningness.
- It is discernment.
- It is comprehension.
- Understanding.
- Observation.
- Instruction.

- Recognition.

1. Knowledge is also prognostication (or the ability to forthtell or to predict according to present indications or signs), just as Daniel did and saved a whole nation of people.
2. Knowledge is surety, it is skill and I love this one, it is "can have".
3. Knowledge is the key that unlocks the doors to our unlimited potential by way of receiving everything that has been hidden from us about our lives.

In order for us to live lives to our fullest potential, we must have:
- Knowledge of what God says is true about us.
- Knowledge of the power of God that is at work on the inside of us.
- Knowledge of how to use that power in order to overcome every obstacle and barrier that comes in our lives.
- Knowledge of how to be productive and able to continue to function while going through trials and even tragedies.

Sidebar: This is why you need a pastor. The pastor has been given to feed you with knowledge and understanding. The Lord said in Jeremiah 3:15, *"And I will give you pastors according to mine heart which shall feed you with knowledge and understanding"*.

Throughout my life I have belonged to three churches. The one that I was born in as a child, the church that I was birthed into when I excepted Christ as my Savior. I stayed at that church for thirty-six years and grew there in many ways until the Lord sent me to plant a church in my hometown which is the church that I founded and currently pastor.

That word pastors in the above scripture has the same meaning in the Hebrew translation as the word feed which means to:

- To guard
- To tend
- To govern
- To rule
- A teacher of virtue
- Shepherd
- Companion
- Friend

You must be fed in order to grow just as a plant needs to be fed nutrients and be watered in order to grow. The purpose of a pastor is to get you through your growth process and to be there for your life. Not just on Sunday morning, but as a regular guide in helping to prepare you for your destiny. A pastor is assigned by the Lord to a particular people or person and should have in them the right word, the right attitude and even the right tools within them to connect their people to their personal callings.

This is why it is so important to be up under the right pastor for your life. In the five years that I have been the Lead Pastor, I have watched people's lives change from welfare to work and school, from living in the projects to renting apartments and from renting to buying homes. I have poured into people's lives to start businesses, write books and plays and so many more things because I am assigned to pastor these particular people and lead them towards their destiny.

We are all expected to grow, to gain more than what we started with. The bible says that even Jesus *"increased in wisdom and stature, and in favour with God and man"*. He increased in:

Stature -   Maturity
Suitable age for anything
Attained state fit for a thing

Favor - Good will
Loving kindness
Delight
Sweetness
Exerting God's influence upon souls
Grace of speech
Thanks

He increased in all these things with God *and* with man. Not only must we grow in the Lord, but we must also grow in relationships with the people that we encounter daily who will also see increase in our lives and God will be glorified.

DEVELOPMENT

Once you have grown to a level of maturity in your life, there will come a time when you become too great to stay where you are. And once you have outgrown that place, that same place that once gave you comfort, provision and stability will become a place of discomfort. If you remain there after you are too great for it to sustain you, it will eventually become your place of enslavement meaning:

- Your place of oppression.
- Your place of exploitation.
- Your place of persecution.
- Your place of suppression.

Please know that it is never God's plan for you to remain in a place where you become a servant to a situation that does not permit you to develop into all that God wants you to be. However, this is not an excuse to bolt saying that your season is up simply because you are not happy with your condition. It is only the Lord that changes the times and the seasons. It is our responsibility to ask for wisdom to know when it is the Lord's timing and when it is not. The children of Israel endured suffering for nearly 450 years until the Lord delivered them in His time.

The bible says, "*And it came to pass in process of time, that the king of Egypt died: and the children of Israel sighed by reason of the bondage, and they cried, and their cry came up unto God by reason of the bondage*". They had grown and increased during their time in Egypt, however because of their bondage, they were not able to make any progress into becoming that great nation of promise. They could not make movement towards their goal, nor could they go any further or higher because they were being oppressed, exploited, persecuted and suppressed. Due to great afflictions they cried out to the Lord and He heard their groaning and raised up Moses to bring them out of captivity so that they could "serve Him in the wilderness".

The Lord hears the cries of our heart and He wants to deliver us out of all our afflictions so that we can be free to serve Him and not be forced to serve a situation. The children of Israel were serving a condition that was not meant to be their place of promise. How many of us are living in situations that we have become slaves to, situations that were once meant for our growth and even for our good. And yet when the Lord's intended purpose was accomplished in us in that situation, we were unable to move on from it because we had become trapped.

It is these types of conditions that the Lord brings us out of with His mighty hand. However, many are so intimidated by how He chooses to bring us out, that we decide that we would rather go back to that situation of bondage and die in it, rather than trust the Lord to progress us forward in our lives.

Forward will always bring abundance and increase into your life, it will always cause you to grow, to become great, to become powerful and do great things. However, you cannot and will not go forward by staying where you are, by going back to what God brought you out of, nor can you achieve abundance and increase in your life without going by way of the wilderness.

We grow in Egypt, but we develop in the wilderness. The wilderness experience comes on the heels of a great spiritual breakthrough. The Children of Israel began their wilderness experience after all the firstborn in Egypt were killed by the death angel. King David's wilderness experience began after he killed Goliath. After Jesus was baptized by John the Baptist and His identity was reveal by the Father from Heaven, the bible says that the Spirit immediately drove him into the wilderness where he fasted and prayed and was tempted of the devil. His wilderness experience was a place of victory over His own flesh, victory over the devil and it was a place of coming into the fullness of what He came to do in the earth.

When we think about the wilderness, we equate it with suffering, temptation and as the place in which we are "stuck" in that is keeping us from the promise. This is far from the truth even though we could end up stuck in the wilderness if we do not learn all that the Lord wants to teach us there.

We may also mistake the wilderness for the promised land and plant ourselves there because the wilderness experience can be a place to expand and be all that you can be.

Here are some truths concerning what the wilderness is:

- The place of development, where you can freely cultivate the land.
- The place where you work out the possibilities for your future without restraints.
- The place where you discover your capabilities.
- The place of expansion of your creativity.
- The place of disclosure, where the invisible is manifested.
- The place of preparation for your purpose.
- Your place of maturing.
- A place of evolution or progressive change.
- A place of freedom to serve the Lord.

- Your place of training (skills and behavior).
- The place of danger.
- The place of temptation (tempted to go back or give up).
- The place of confrontation (where you must confront yourself).
- The place of revelation (where the Lord reveals to you, who He is to you).
- A place of solitude (being alone with God).

The children of Israel had to rely on the Egyptians for all their needs. In the wilderness you are forced to rely on the Lord for provision, protection and instruction. It is there that you will learn that He is the one who sustains you and that He alone is your source, your protection and your identity. You will also learn that He is the one who nourishes you with the two basic things that you need in order to live:

1. Water - of the word
2. Manna - bread of His presence

Being alone with the Lord will also develop the trust factor in you where you will learn how to trust the Lord without outside interferences, influences or factors. Below are three ways in which trust will be developed in your alone season with the Lord while in the wilderness.

1. In new situations and new circumstances.
2. In places that are uncharted - unexplored, unfamiliar, unknown.
3. In that place where He must continue to do the "new".

CHAPTER 10

Rejection, The Road To Purpose

Rejection doesn't just hurt our feelings as some may think. But rejection deeply touches the soul and affects us spiritually, physically and emotionally often for a lifetime.

Rejection comes in many forms and can vary in strength, from simply ignoring a person to public embarrassments, being passive aggressive, criticism and ostracizing people. If a person does not pass the standards, tests and evaluations that people place on them, we will socially and emotionally downgrade them to the level that we want to place them in using physical, emotional and psychological tactics.

Rejection is a form of identity assassination that helps to pervert the way a person sees themselves. This is why it is so important to accept the person even though one may accept or reject what they do. This way we don't destroy their identity or their sense of self-worth.

People who suffer the effects of rejection do so mainly because they place their value in someone's acceptance of who they are and what they do. But once we learn that we are valuable because God has made us that way, the opinions of people will become less and less important to our general wellbeing. I have written a chapter on "Knowing Your Worth" in this book, which will help you to find ways to discover the value that you already possess in Christ.

So, what does the word reject actually mean?

It means to: disapprove or to refuse to support.

Luke 9:5 says, " *And whosoever will not receive (accept) you, when ye go out of that city, shake off the very dust from your feet for a testimony against them*".
Very often, when people reject us, it is not us that they are rejecting, but it is what is in us that they have a problem with. And it is that gift, that talent, that characteristic, that trait that they don't understand, that they can't

understand, that they don't agree with or they have decided does not fit into their mold, that they are refusing to accept.

In the above scripture, dust represents man and his fleshly nature which is at the root of rejection. What this scripture is saying is that some of us are still carrying around the dust of someone's rejection of us and we have not let it go and made a clean break from it.

What the Lord was saying to His disciples in this passage is, if they don't want to receive me through you, shake the dust off as a testimony against them. Once they (the disciples) released those people from their lives, the bible says, *"they were filled with joy and with the Holy Ghost"*.

What a lesson to learn! If we would simply release people from our lives who reject us by walking away and not letting the rejection cling to us, we can be filled with joy. You are not expected to remain bound to people who do not want you.

When Jesus was experiencing the extreme rejection that led Him to the cross, the bible says that *"He went on for the joy that was set before Him, enduring the cross and despising the shame"*. He understood that even though it was rejection that drove him to his destiny, he could not allow the effect that the rejection could have had on His mind to cause Him to sin and forfeit the plan and purpose that the Lord had for the salvation of mankind.

Jesus knew that even though the rejection would be harsh, it was still the road to His purpose. Jesus said, *"but first I must be rejected. They must refuse to accept me. They will lie on me, they will mock me and spit in my face"*. He also said to his own disciple, Peter, *"You will deny knowing me three times. They will choose a murderer over me and condemn me to be crucified"*, they will even try to kill me even before I get to the cross. But thanks be to God their rejection of Him, didn't keep Him from His purpose but, it fulfilled it, it completed everything that God said about Him and it caused the will of God to come to pass.

Very often that same rejection that we are struggling with has been permitted to come into our lives to push us to our purpose. Therefore, when the rejection comes it is imperative that you let God be strong in you and protect who you are and the purpose for which you are here and not let the rejection coming from people kill your destiny.

When you are being rejected, it is your responsibility to remind yourself of who you are and of God's plan and purpose for who you are. Know that your identity is in Him and your identity is connected to your purpose. When a thing is identified, it can then be correctly used for the purpose in which it was intended. People often reject other people because they don't have a clear understanding of who that person is, and what their intended purpose is in their lives.

The Lord told Jeremiah the prophet, "*Before I formed thee* (before I purposed you, before I said what I was going to use you to do) *in the belly I knew thee;* (I knew exactly who you were, I gave you your identity). *And before thou cometh forth out of the womb, I sanctified thee and I ordained thee a prophet unto the nations*". God talked about both Jeremiah's identity and purpose in that text so that there would be no confusion when Jeremiah and his ministry became rejected by people.

You will never escape rejection of one kind or another. As a matter of fact, the bible gives a woe unto those who are loved by all. If you aren't being rejected, perhaps you are not making much of an impact to be noticeable.

In this life you will quickly discover that everyone is not for you and will not be supportive of what the Lord has spoken about you. You may not discover who is or is not for you until you begin to do something major in your life. It is at that time that you will begin to discover who people really are as the hearts of those whom you are connected to will be revealed.

Everyone in your life is not connected to your future in the way that you think they are. There will come a time that you will have to learn how to release yourself from those who are rejecting you, who mean you no good and then overcome the hurt of being betrayed by those who you were once connected to.

In order to help you way before the rejection comes, you must begin to categorize the people that are in your life especially when it comes to your dreams and God's plan for your life. Even the nastiest person in your life is there to help you to get to your destination. The Lord may use that person for one single thing to move you forward or they may be there for an extended time to help you progress but not there for a lifetime.

Some people are connected to you to the end. They have been assigned to your life all the way through and to take up the mantle that you leave behind when the Lord upgrades you into the life to come.

Others may not be in your life permanently and that is alright. They may be there to help you grow and get through the rough stages of your life. They may be there to share in an assignment that God has for you for a period. But then there may come a time of separation when the Lord begins to move you in His perfect will for your life and the perfect will for that person's life is no longer connected to you.

In certain instances when the separation will be a difficult one because of a particular bond between both parties, the break must be unambiguous. To achieve this, the Lord will allow the rejection of one party to be deeply felt to ensure that the parties will not reconnect until His purpose is accomplished. Joseph was rejected in that way by his own brothers, but the rejection was only to position Joseph to fulfill the mission of preserving Israel many years later.

When it comes to categorizing people for the sake of peace in your life, and to identify those who have the potential of rejecting you, here are three quick negative traits to watch for. These are not the only traits good or bad, but I want to mention these particular traits to watch out for.

1. Watch out for people who have never supported you.

Even though you have done for them, when your turn comes to be in the forefront, they will refuse to support you. You can help these types of people and be there even in their roughest situations, but rarely will they be there for you in yours. If they have never supported you, they will certainly not support your dream either and will do whatever they can to make sure others follow their lead.

2. Be careful of people who refuse to celebrate with you.

Now, you should not be one who is looking for affirmation from man by any means or one who "expects to be celebrated for the things that you do". You should always be willing to do even if no one says good job or pats you on the back. But it is best to keep a close eye on those who never say anything good about you. People who never compliment you, who rarely show any type of happiness for accomplishments that you achieve outside of them fit into this category. They are happy for you if what you are doing is enhancing their lives, but they aren't happy for you if you are celebrated outside of them.

3. Watch out for those who are secretly jealous of you. Jealousy is a sneaky thing and it can manifest in different ways, including the ones listed above.

But the jealous person is the most dangerous of all. They secretly want what you have or what is in you and are angry at you because they think that you are taking away from them. Instead of them understanding that what they have in them is just as valuable as what you have, or knowing that what the Lord has for you has no detrimental effect on them, they will do whatever they can to ruin your reputation, and try to make you feel and look inferior in front of others in order to discredit you so that others will reject you as well. These types of people will seek out someone else who has a problem with you and befriend them so that they can have more "power" to come up against you.

They will find you useful if you do their bidding, but they will do whatever they can to keep you submissive to them so that they can control you. If they control you, they will make themselves great through you.

If jealous people are permitted to stay in your life for an extended period and you do not deal with them by culling them out of your life first, they will eventually do whatever they must do to permanently shut you down.

The bible says, *"Jealousy is the rage of a man: therefore he will not spare in the day of vengeance. He will not regard any ransom; neither will he rest content, though thou givest many gifts"*. It doesn't matter what good you do for a person who is jealous of you, they will never be satisfied with what you do for them and they will never be willing to accept you no matter how great the thing is that you do for them or give to them. They will have no pity, no compassion and no gentleness for you if there ever comes a time to take vengeance against you.

Therefore, you must guard what God is saying and doing in your life, because you won't really know who is for you until you open your mouth and begin to talk about your dreams and your destiny. Joseph's brothers were already secretly jealous of him, but they didn't try to kill him until he started sharing his dreams with them.

Everyone is not going to understand you, and everyone is not going to like you. Even your closes friends and family members may have a disagreement with you that will change their entire stance towards you. No matter what you may try to do to reconcile that relationship, they may not want to reconnect with you forcing you to have to move on without them.

So, what do you do once people are removed from your life or when those that you trusted reject you and throw you in the pit?

1. You forgive. It may have taken Joseph years to forgive his brothers the bible doesn't say, but when the time came that they needed help, Joseph's heart was already prepared to be a blessing to them. But here this, forgiveness does not have to take time. The only time it needs is the time that it takes for you to change your mind.

2. Use what is in you in prison (that foreign place that you were thrust into because of the rejection) knowing that the same qualities that caused you to be rejected will be the same qualities that will get you out of your feelings of low self-worth and bring you before great men. Joseph was no longer under the influence of his family's opinion, so he was free to be him as the opportunities came to do so.

3. Allow the Lord to transform you by the renewing of your mind. When Joseph's brother's saw him, he was so changed until they didn't even recognize him. Let your mind be so far from your past, your past hurts, disappointments and betrayals until those whom the Lord sends back into your life, will not recognize the new you. You should be so changed that you are eager to bless those that curse you, pray for those who despitefully use you and serve those who in the past rejected you.

If your self-image is poor stemming from what you have allowed yourself to receive from the people that have rejected you, it will come out in the decisions that you make for your life. You will pass up opportunities for growth and advancement, you will never take risks for fear of how people will receive you and you will live a life of mediocracy doing just enough to get by each day.

CHAPTER 11

Abuse

Abuse in any definition of the word is not the Lord's plan for anyone's life. The Lord did not call you to stay in a situation in which you are being threatened, one in which your life is in danger, where you are being exploited, controlled or in bondage to another person or to a situation or where you find yourself being victimized on a regular basis.

I am going to put a pin right here so that I can talk a little bit about my qualifications to speak on abuse. I am a survivor of domestic violence and have been removed from the situation for close to thirty years. I married a man over thirty-five years ago with whom I had three children with, one prior to marriage and two more that were born after we were married. I suffered verbal, physical, mental, emotional, sexual, and financial abuse until I left the marriage after eight long years with three young children. When I had finally had enough, I began to empower myself in preparation to leave. When the Lord made the opportunity available, I went into a shelter for battered women with my children and stayed there for an entire month. It was the best thing that I have ever done for myself.

It took me several months to plan my exit once I had gotten to the point to where I knew that I was better than what I had allowed myself to live with. Therefore, I very much understand that leaving any abusive situation is not something to be lightly considered, nor is it easy to just get up and leave as some suppose. There are many who have attempted to be free from an abuser and have lost their lives in the process. What worked for me, may not work for you in that every case and every abuser is different.

Once you begin to empower yourself, your abuser may become even more controlling to keep you in check. If you are careful in planning your next steps with precision, wisdom, secrecy and the help of one or two trusted confidants, you will be able to move forth as needed.

I never recommend telling your abuser that you are leaving or giving him/her any clues to what you are planning, nor tell him where you are going, ever! If you are in fear for your life, please make sure that you work with the judicial system as I did and with your local law enforcement team to make sure that your safety is secured.

Silence is key to a safe escape even if you must be silent for years concerning your whereabouts until you are one hundred percent sure that your abuser is no longer concerned about you. Starting a new life in a new state or a new country if need be is better than the risk of being fatally injured. I am grateful to have come out of my situation with my life, but I personally know women who did not.

Abuse is all about power and control. If a person is able to position themselves in a place of power over you, then they can control you. There are many people who are under the control of another and that person has never laid a hand on them. However, they have established themselves as the only voice and as the only one who loves them and have used isolation to bring the person under subjection to them. Abuse can be blatant, and it can be subtle, each are just as dangerous.

In my case, I gave the power of my life over to my abuser when I granted him access to my weaknesses. Some may become angry at this next statement, but I believe that there is a root of weakness in a person who finds themselves in an abusive situation. These weaknesses may be dormant in a person's life for decades until the right person comes along who is able to gain access into us through an opening and then use our weakness for their benefit.

Personally, I saw the signs that my ex-husband was an abuser before we said, "I do" and I ignored them. We often ignore signs and allow people in our space that should not have the type of access to who we are that we give them.

Later in this chapter, we will talk about the warning signs that many tend to ignore until it is too late. The best defense is in the offense in this case. Know the signs of an abuser before you begin any relationship and do not ignore the signs. They will not go away with love and pampering nor will you be able to change that person. You cannot change an abuser.

There are many types of abuse. Below I have listed a few of them.
- Physical abuse
- Sexual Abuse

- Emotional/ Verbal
- Mental/Psychological Abuse
- Financial Abuse
- Spiritual Abuse

Abuse is not limited to domestic abuse; however, I am focusing on that type of abuse for the sake of this lesson. Domestic abuse is something that is rarely discussed in churches. Many years ago when I was young in the Lord, I remember seeing several young girls on different occasions come to church with battered faces. Each came and took their position in the choir with no one saying anything or doing anything about what they saw. Everyone acted as if they did not see it and the young girls also behaved as if the abuse was a normal part of their day.

Often when an abused person who may be married has an opportunity to sit with a leader to talk about their situation, they are told to go back home and "submit", to stay married to their abuser. They are told that God hates divorce. They may even be told that if they divorce, they cannot remarry except to that same abusive spouse or be condemned to live a life of loneliness until that abuser drops dead.

And because we hang our hats on one or two passages which are taken out of context or taught without the cultural references or historical knowledge, we put an even greater yoke around the neck of people who are already living a life of bondage and fear.

This is one of the reasons why I stayed so long in my own abusive situation. I thought I had made my bed, so now I must lay in it, forever. But when my mind was changed by the gospel of Jesus Christ and I understood the depth of the love that He had for me, the depth of His mercy over my mistakes and the plans and promises that He had for my future, my mind was freed so that I could go and live a life of peace and purpose. *"There is therefore now no condemnation to those who are in Christ Jesus, who walk not after the flesh, but after the spirit. For the law of the spirit of life in Christ Jesus hath made me free from the law of sin and death"*.

It is also my firm belief, that we as leaders fall short and fail the people that we are called to shepherd by not providing shelters, counselors, or partnering with local law enforcement and other agencies to provide safety and help to those who are suffering from abuse.

Now, let's talk a little about how you can know if you are being abused by someone in your life. Begin by asking yourself these questions:

Do you feel belittled or put down on a regular basis? _____
Are you afraid to voice your opinion for fear of ostracism? _____
Do you feel uncomfortable or afraid around a person? _____
Is someone controlling your ability to progress in life? _____
Are you being shamed for a decision that you have made? _____
Are you being pressured or forced to do things against your will? _____
Are you being threatened with some sort of harm on a regular basis? _____
Is someone using intimidation tactics to keep you "in line"? _____
Are someone's passive aggressive actions causing you emotional distress? ___
Is someone controlling where you go or spying on you? _____
Are you slowing being isolated from others? _____

As I stated earlier, abuse has many faces and shows up in many genres and is not limited to domestic violence or child abuse nor is abuse confined to the home environment. But abuse is also found in the house of God.

It is rare to find someone that has not been hurt or felt abused by someone in church. However, the phrase "church hurt" is being coined by so many who have been hurt by a person or a group of people within a specific church but what they are experiencing is not necessarily abuse.

The house of God is full of people who have not been fully delivered or set free from past hurts. These same people came with an expectation of finding the Lord amongst "perfect people". And when they find out that the people that they expected to be perfect are also flawed, and do or say something to hurt them, they find it difficult to overcome the hurt and leave, calling it "church hurt".

But, I am still going to touch on the subject of abuse in the church. You will see from the list below that many of the abuses found in the "world" are common place in the church as well. This lets us know that there is much work to be done in all of our lives.

Sexual Abuse: When a leader uses his/her position to coerce a member to have sex with them saying that they must do so in order to move ahead in ministry. The leader may also say that the member is considered special, therefore this sexual relationship will seal their special bond. As always, they are told to "keep it a secret" so that the abuse can continue.

Manipulation: Keeping one from leaving a ministry by telling them that they will not make it if they do. The person who is contemplating moving on is made to feel as if though the leader is their only way to salvation and if they leave, they are cutting off their "life source". Leaders may make people feel as if though their life is owed to the leader because of all that the leader has poured into that person over the years. They will use this to try to "guilt" a person into staying even though the Lord may have told that person to move on.

People are also manipulated into given exorbitant amounts of money for special programs or offerings by being made to feel as if though the word that they received will not apply to their lives if they do not "sow" into it. A leader may embarrass a member who cannot give as others can and make them feel as if though they must figure out a way to give even if they must give up their bill money to do so.

Fear: Making people afraid to voice their opinion or speak contrary to the leadership. If they disagree then they are "touching" God's anointed and will be "struck" down for harming the prophet. Openly criticizing a church member over the pulpit is a fear tactic. If it is done to one member, then the rest of the church will be afraid that it will happen to them if they come against the leadership. A leader should never talk about what a member has brought to them in confidence over the pulpit nor should they correct a member over the pulpit by calling that person out. This is abuse at its finest.

Open rebuke is good for the soul, but humiliation and embarrassment is a killer.

CHAPTER 12

I'm Over It

I wanted to add this chapter after our talk on abuse because the only way for many of us to come out of abusive situations is to finally say, "I am over it, I have had enough" and then act to remove oneself from the situation permanently.

Often, we never get to the place of saying that we are done and meaning it with our heart. We say that we are done with a thing, but do we really mean it?

When I was in that abusive marriage, I would daily talk about the situation to anyone who would listen. Each and every time I would reiterate the same stories, the same emotions that I was feeling, the same anger and the same lie about "having enough of it". I would even pack my bags at least once every other month and leave with my children, only to return the next day to that same abusive marriage. Why? Because I wasn't really over it yet. I wasn't sick and tired enough to do something about it, I just liked talking about it more.

It took eight years for me to finally get to the place of no longer talking about it but doing something about it. When I finally had a made-up mind that I was done, I was done, and I began to position myself for an exit. Once I began to put my plan into motion, I knew there was no going back to simply talking about it.

It is amazing how the smallest step or a single thought that sticks, can empower a person for a lifetime. Change begins in the mind first. If you think on something long enough, it will get down in your heart and move you to action.

It was all about survival by the time I had made up my mind that I was over it. I was now in "us" mode. Making sure that I and my children would forever be safe from the abuse became my priority. He had threatened to kill me several times over the years, but it wasn't until he tried to kill all of us by driving recklessly around blind curves in the dense fog at close to eighty miles an hour, that I knew I had to get me and my children out of that situation or we would all soon be dead.

I immediately began to disconnect myself from anything that would keep me attached to him or that marriage. I had never taken control of my own life in that way before and as frightening as it was to do the things that I needed to do, it felt good to finally have a sense of control over my own life.

"Over it" does not always come to a person overnight. It is very often a process that comes after a long period of enduring the suffering. There are somethings in life that it takes longer for certain types of people to be done with. Some people will not get there until they have had their fill of it even though their suffering is almost unbearable to them. Some will not be over it until they are able to conclude it on their own, no matter how much we try to convince them otherwise. They must make it up in their own mind.

A made-up mind means that the person has made a final decision after a period of vacillating or after a period where there was an inability to take a stand. A person with a made-up mind is a person who's talk is now backed up by actions.

In the book of John 5:2, the bible reads, *"And a certain man who was at the pool of Bethesda which had an infirmity thirty and eight years"*. In the seventh verse of this same chapter he is called the impotent man or the powerless man. That word impotent means, someone who purposely abstains from the use of his strength.

Many of us are weak with intent and don't even know it. We are intentionally and subconsciously sabotaging our own lives with our weak thinking and blaming the situation and others for why we can't come out of it.

That word impotent also means one who has no reason to prove his strength. Because many of us have lost hope or think there is nothing better for us than what we are currently dealing with, we won't try to take control of our lives. The bible says in Proverbs 13:12, *"Hope deferred makes the heart sick"*. When you have waited for change for a long period of time and you don't see it, the heart begins to give up believing that change is never going to come. Your outlook becomes bleak and you begin to settle in that situation using different coping mechanisms just so that you can "deal" with it.

The loss of hope is a dangerous place to be in. However, that scripture goes on to say, *"But when the desire comes, it is a tree of life"*. When you begin to long for better, to change your mind and set your sights on who you really are in Christ, life begins to happen!

Impotent also means one who is weak in faith, one who is weak in feeling and conviction about what is lawful or allowable for him to do, or for him to have or do with his or her own life. A weak person does not believe that they can have peace, they don't believe that it is okay for them to live an abundant life or that it is lawful for them to be made whole. Jesus asked the man; *will thou be made whole?* Do you even want to be over this? Haven't you had enough of this yet? Don't you want better?

But the man, like many of us, began to make excuses. Whenever you are weak, you make excuses as to why you are still in a condition. No man was there to put me in the pool, it's their fault. I tried but I couldn't do it by myself. And he stayed in that condition thirty-eight years playing the victim.

When you are a victim, you see yourself as powerless to change your condition. We use the phrase, "victim of abuse" or "victim of domestic violence", victim of some sort of illness, which puts a label on the person as being unable to gain the upper hand in that situation. However, certain people only need knowledge on how to change their situation. Once they get that knowledge, they will change their lives forever.

Here is a list of characteristics of someone with a victim's mentality. Read the list and begin to ask yourself if you identify with at least more than one item on the list:

- You blame others because you are not happy
- You think that everything and everyone is against you
- You always see the bad in people and situations
- You refuse to take responsibility for your role in anything
- You think others are purposely trying to hurt you
- You believe you're the only one being targeted for mistreatment
- You can't accept constructive criticism from anyone
- You revel in the pity of others
- You surround yourself with other miserable people
- You always see the glass half empty and never half full
- You refuse any attempts at self-examination
- You constantly put yourself down

For many years, I saw myself as a victim. How I saw myself, made me feel as if though I couldn't change my condition.

This is why the Lord became so angry at the Children of Israel when they made excuses why they could not go into the promised land. They said, in the book of Numbers, 13:33, *"and we are in our own sight as grasshoppers, and so we are in their sight"*. It didn't matter to them that the Lord had been with them, nor did they remember all the miracles that He had performed in their lives. Neither did they consider promises that He had spoken to them over and over again. They saw themselves as small and weak. They believed that they had no power to take what already belonged to them. Because of this, they did not receive the promise even though it was right there for them to walk into.

But this is what I love about the woman in the bible with the issue of blood. She refused to be a victim and did all that she could to do something about her situation even down to spending her last dime. The bible says in Luke 8:43, *And a woman having an issue of blood twelve years, which had spent all her living upon physicians, neither could be healed of any*. Here is the best part, *"For she said within herself, if I may but touch his garment, I shall be whole"*. In other words, she began to empower herself in her mind first.

This woman had been bleeding for twelve years straight. She had an issue of blood meaning, a flux of blood or an abnormal discharge of blood. Any condition or circumstance that we hold on to that is contrary to the word of God is abnormal. Abuse is abnormal, low self-esteem is abnormal, rejection is abnormal, unforgiveness is abnormal, living in lack is abnormal. Shall I continue? And because we have had this issue for many years, it has made us weak and powerless and victims of the situation.

This issue affected her whole entire life. It's one thing to have an issue that doesn't complicate your life, but this thing not only complicated her life, it had power over her entire life. Her issue became psychological, physical, emotional, spiritual and social and it was relentless for twelve years, never letting up, no end in sight even though she tried to get some help by doing what she knew to do.

But the bible says that she said within herself, "I'm over this". She began to empower herself by saying, "If I am going to be made whole, I am going to have to act".

Well how do I empower myself to go from victim to victor?

Change your prospective about what is happening in your life and then choose to do something about it. The Lord has already made provisions for you to do something about any situation that you may be dealing with by giving you the power of choice. You can either choose to do something about it, or choose to do nothing about it, but the choice will be yours and yours alone. However, the Lord always helps us to make the right choice by giving us the answer. Choose life.

The four lepers in 2 Kings 7:3 said, *"Why sit we here until we die"*? They understood that they had a choice concerning their situation. If we stay here we are going to die here. We know that there is nothing more for us at this place we are in. There is no provision, no help, no future. So why would we stay here. They assessed their situation and came to the conclusion that they needed to do something.

But they also thought if we go, we are going to die there too. Fear keeps us from making a decision because we don't know what will happen to us if we choose to change our situation. However, they made the right choice to go and went in spite of the fear and gained a decisive victory.

The bible speaks of a woman named Tamar who, on the other hand, made the choice to do nothing about her situation. In 2 Samuel 13th chapter the bible says, *"And it came to pass after this, that Absalom the son of David had a fair sister, whose name was Tamar; and Amnon the son of David loved her. And Amnon was so vexed, that he fell sick for his sister Tamar; for she was a virgin; and Amnon thought it hard for him to do anything to her. But Amnon had a friend, whose name was Jonadab, the son of Shimeah David's brother: and Jonadab was a very subtil man"*.

Jonadab helped Amnon to scheme so that he could get close to Tamar. The scheme went as planned however, Amnon thought Tamar would fall for him and give herself to him, but when she didn't, he raped her. Amnon quickly felt guilt for his behavior, but instead of repenting, assuming responsibility, doing what was right before God, he hated Tamar, had her thrown out of the house and then had his servants bolt the door so that she could never get back in.

The bible goes on to say, *"And Tamar put ashes on her head, and rent her garment of divers colours that was on her, and laid her hand on her head, and* went on crying. When Tamar's father David heard about it he became "very angry" (2 Samuel 13:21) but does nothing about it.

But Absalom her brother said unto her, "Hath Amnon thy brother been with thee? but hold now thy peace, my sister: he is thy brother; regard not this thing".

When Amnon raped her, he took her life from her. And on top of it, her father David did nothing about it. It seemed like Absalom was the only one who cared about what happened to her, but he told her to be quiet about it.

Here this, it may seem like people are the answer to your problems. However, people cannot and will not handle your life in the way that God has already planned for you to handle it. They will tell you what to do based on their own experiences, but do not know the plan that the Lord has for you in that experience. The Lord already has a plan in place to move you forward, to advance your life, to deal with your hurts, disappointments and grief. He has a plan to handle your crisis and most of us fail in a crisis because we fail to follow the emergency protocol! Instead, we listen to bad counsel that often worsens our condition.

In Jewish culture, an unmarried woman who was not a virgin had little to no hope of survival in the world. Therefore, the marriage of a raped woman by the one who raped her was commanded by the Lord as a protection for that woman. The Lord clearly said in His word that the rapist must marry her and he could never divorce her for any reason. This was to ensure that she would live a protected life and be taken care of throughout it.

However, if the woman who was raped was already married, then the rapist would be put to death because she didn't need to be sustained, because she already had a husband.

Tamar knew this. This is why she said, "this evil in sending me away is greater than the other that thou didst unto me". But the bible says, "But he would not hearken unto her."

So, she went away and told her brother who eventually killed Amnon years later. But this did nothing whatsoever for her life, as a matter of fact, it made a bad thing worse. Because Amnon was dead, any rights that she had to be married, have children, possibly be loved for real, and live a full life after such a terrible thing, died with him.

We allow people, to do whatever they want to do in our life. They say what they want, treat us any old kind of way and we seldom make a ruckus and say, "I don't have to accept this because I know my rights. I am going to take charge of my life and do something about it myself".

Most of us don't know our rights nor do we even try to get an understanding of what is or is not allowable in our lives, or we hand our lives over to people who really can't care for us the way that the Lord can.

But, Tamar knew her rights and made a conscious choice to do nothing about what was done to her .

Luke 11:7-8 says, *"And he from within shall answer and say, Trouble me not: the door is now shut, and my children are with me in bed; I cannot rise and give thee. I say unto you, Though he will not rise and give him, because he is his friend, yet because of his importunity he will rise and give him as many as he needeth"* . In other words, he may say no because he is not bound to you, however, because of your importunity, your boldness and utter disregard for the fact that he said no, he will have to give you what you ask for.

Even though Amnon threw her out and locked the doors, she could have banged on the door and forced him to do what he legally needed to do to right the wrong that he did to her. Even if he refused to answer, she could have gone to her father and told him that she wanted Amnon to marry her as he should, but she did not.

She should have told Absalom, "I appreciate you wanting to help me, but no, I won't be quiet, this is my battle and I got this. I am the one who has been violated, who has been abused and hurt and rejected and shamed and thrown away. Therefore, I am going to take possession of what is rightfully mine based on what was done to me".

We may also wonder why David, as the king, didn't do something after Absalom told him what happened to Tamar. He got angry but, did nothing.

Because Tamar never went to her father herself, he could not intervene in something that only Tamar could do something about. If she didn't take control of her life and fully exercise her rights herself, his hands were tied.

We often wait for the Lord to do something about our situations, but He cannot and will not unless we have done all that we by rights can do. *"So Tamar remained desolate in her brother Absalom's house".*

CHAPTER 13

Dealing with Offences

The bible says in Matthew 18:7, "Woe unto the world because of offences! for it must needs be that offences come; but woe to that man by whom the offence cometh"!

We must have a clear understanding that we will never escape being offended by people. The scripture clearly says it's coming. But offences are not come to hurt or harm you even though that may have been the intended purpose of the one who offended you, but the Lord allows offences to come so that they may build good character in you.

Offences are defined as an annoyance or resentment brought about by a perceived insult to or disregard for oneself or one's standards or principles. It is a feeling or displeasure that comes with a cause.

The enemy will use that offence as a stumbling block that has the potential to trip you up or cause you to fall. He knows how we will react to the offence based on what he has learned by observing us throughout our life. He also knows that there is a deeper problem that was left untouched that caused us to be offended. His plan is to cause you to focus on the offence so that you are never free from the fundamental condition that caused you to be offended.

Being offended is a symptom. It is the manifestation of a condition and a sign of the existence of something in us that is undesirable to the Lord.

As in the natural, the symptoms of the offence increase in severity when the underlying condition is not treated.

1. There is displeasure.
2. Your feelings are hurt.
3. The offence angers you.
4. It builds up resentment in you.

5. The offence causes you to become bitter.
6. Eventually it causes you to sin.

We waste time dealing with the symptoms and not the cause of the symptoms. Often, we think that a problem is solved because we got rid of the symptoms, when in reality we were simply masking the root problem in exchange for "feeling better".

Jesus never dealt with the symptoms. When he saw the demoniac he went straight to the root of the man's condition, *"What is your name? My name is legion for we are many"*.

When He encountered the woman at the well. *"Where is your husband"?* Even when correcting His own disciple Peter, *"Get thee behind me, Satan"*. He always looked deeper past the surface manifestation of a condition and found the root of the problem.

Perhaps something happened in your childhood that was triggered by how someone spoke to you that caused you to feel offended. What happened to you as a child is the root cause, not what the person said to you or how they said it.

Roots have things attached to it, thoughts, feelings, propensities, or tendencies. Therefore, if the root problem is uprooted, then all of the other issues attached to it will also be removed. This is why the Lord must allow the offences of people to gain an entrance into our lives. Offences cause us to discover the inner contents of our heart so that we can properly deal with what is uncovered by the offence.

Lamentations 3:40 says, "*Let us search and try our ways, and turn again to the LORD*". That word try means to examine intimately and to penetrate or gain entrance to. As uncomfortable and hurtful as the offence may be, " *it must needs be*", as the bible says, that offences come.

And yet, offences rarely come from people that we interact with on a casual basis, but offences generally come from those that we are in close and frequent contact with.

And because there was a level of vulnerability in you because of past hurts that have not healed, a high level of trust that you previously had with the offender and an opening that was created for the offense by situations or circumstances, you were left either physically or emotionally harmed by someone that you did not expect to offend you.

One of the hardest things for us to get over is an offence afflicted upon us by someone who is close to us. Here is a short list of offenders along with an offence that may have come through a door of vulnerability.

- A spouse who has been unfaithful to you
- A parent that walked away from you
- A relative that abused or molested you
- A mother that did not love you like you thought she should
- Friends that may have betrayed you

This is why David said, *"For it was not an enemy that reproached me; then I could have borne it: neither was it he that hated me that did magnify himself against me; then I would have hid myself from him: But it was thou, a man mine equal, my guide, and mine acquaintance. We took sweet counsel together, and walked unto the house of God in company"*.

When we are offended in these types of ways by people in whom we have at one time trusted and communed with, it is difficult for us to focus on ourselves. We feel that it was the offender's fault, because they betrayed the trust factor. Therefore, it is their responsibility to make amends for the offense. We begin to see the offender as someone that deserves fire to be sent down from heaven to consume them and everything that they are associated with because our hurt is so deep. Sadly enough, many would rather see them burn in hell than to forgive or get over the offence.

Howbeit, being offended by someone is never an excuse to get out of the will of God for your life. But we must also learn how to see the offence as God's way to teach us how to love people the way that He loves us and to forgive even when it seems impossible to forgive.

Let's talk about the dreaded word, forgive.

That word forgive in the bible means:

- To send away
- To let go
- To disregard
- Not to discuss now
- To keep no longer

- To order to go to another place
- To give up a debt

Unforgiveness is a surefire way to hold on to an offence, to keep us bound to our past and keep us from moving forward with purpose. But more importantly it keeps us connected to the offender.

Unforgiveness is a spiritual poison that we drink expecting the other person that we are angry with to die. It poisons our mind, our soul and even our body and causes everything from mental depression, to health problems such as cancer, fibromyalgia and arthritis.

"Let's Talk" about the people that you know that offended you and the reason why you were offended by them. We will start by being honest with ourselves and making a list of those people along with what they did or said that offended you.

_____
_____
_____
_____
_____
_____
_____
_____
_____
_____
_____

Now, let's connect those offences with the root cause. Make a list of what may have happened in your past that triggered the feelings or the memory that you had when you were offended by those on your previous list.

_____
_____
_____
_____
_____
_____
_____
_____
_____
_____

_____

_____

_____

_____

When we fully understand what it was in our past that triggered the offense, then we can better move towards forgiving the offender. Forgiveness does not release you from the effects of the hurt, but it certainly is the only way to begin the process toward the road to recovery.

Be assured that letting go of our past and present offences may not be easy to do and it may take time as well as conscious intentional thinking to function in such a high capacity of moral character. Does it mean that you are morally corrupt if you struggle with forgiveness? The answer is emphatically, "No". But it does mean that you have some maturing to do in order to walk in the level of spiritual authority and power that Jesus walked in. After all, He displayed the highest level of moral character when He forgave the entire world for our past, present and future offences toward Him.

"How do I begin the process?", you may ask. By learning how to replace your feelings of hurt, anger, bitterness, with love, empathy and compassion. This is accomplished by:

- Praying for those that have caused you to be offended.
- Thinking thoughts of good will towards the offender.

But, herein lies the struggle and the questions that are very often in our hearts that keep us bound to the offender.

- Can I give up my will to hate you when you lied on me?
- Can I give up my desire to lash out at you with my tongue when you mistreated me?
- Can I give up my desire to stay home just to avoid you?
- Can I risk you thinking that I am weak, because I decide to love you anyway?
- Can I hold myself in position, can I stay who I am, when my offender walks into a room and never flinch, bat an eye or cringe on the inside?
- How can I call you my friend again after I have been offended by you in the worst way?

- How do I move on if the one that hurt me in the past is no longer alive and I can't confront them with my hurt?

In order to answer these questions and some others that you may want to ask, here are eight steps to help you on your way to wholeness.

1. Acknowledge that you are hurt. Don't try to be tough and act as if though nothing affects you. If you are hurt say so but say so to the Lord! Refrain from gossiping about your hurt or telling the story to gain sympathy from others. It only perpetuates the hurt as you relive it each time you talk about it. If you must tell someone, tell someone who will pray with you and give you good counsel according to the word of God and will keep your words in confidence.

2. Look inside yourself and honestly try to discern what in your past caused you to be hurt the way that you were hurt. Jesus said, *"Hereafter I will not talk much with you, for the prince of the world cometh and hath nothing in me"*. Meaning, we can't be hurt or offended when there is nothing in us to trigger a reaction to the offense. We must always examine ourselves by the word of God to see what manner of man we are and then deal with whatever we find that the enemy can use against us.

3. Try to see the offender as God sees them. Realize that the one that hurt you has most likely been hurt by someone else themselves. If you see the offender as flawed and in need of prayer, this will give rise to compassion in your heart. This does not mean that you condone the wrong that they did to you, but you will have a better understanding of what caused them to do what they did, and it will keep you from seeing yourself as a victim.

4. Get the focus on you. Recognize your role in the offence. We rarely come away from these types of situations smelling like a rose. "I didn't do anything to them, how could they treat me like that", cannot be your response. You must make sure that you did not have a bad attitude towards that person, secretly gossip about them, or treat them in some manner that may cause them to come for you. What could you have said or done differently? If you are not at fault and

blame free, focus on what you can do to use the offence to empower yourself or others.

5. When you begin to replay the offence, shift your mind to a place of peace in God. Redirect your thoughts to think right thoughts. *"Think on whatsoever things are true, honest, just, pure, lovely and of good report along with virtuous and praise worthy things"*. You are not only what you eat, but you are what you think.

6. Tell yourself that it is ok to be ok. If people have walked out of your life or have hurt you to the point that the relationship cannot be repaired, learn how to find a new normal and be "good" without them. If they could so easily offend you and then walk out of your life, then perhaps the relationship was not as you imagined it to be. Move on and form new bonds and live. A life well-lived is not lived as a form of revenge on others as it is commonly taught, but it is the only way to please the Lord with whom we have to do. Focus on your mission and purpose in life and put your energy into accomplishing those things that you have been called to do.

7. Pray. Prayer is the key that releases compassion in your heart. Compassion is not just love, but it is love in action and it is what causes you to do good to those that have offended you. As you pray for your offender, the Lord will begin to heal your heart. When you pray for the offender it generates a love for that person that is supernatural in nature and you will find yourself genuinely concerned about their spiritual wellbeing.

8. Reconcile any relationship that can be mended. If you do your part to make sure that you are not to blame for a relationship that cannot be repaired, the Lord will be pleased. Earlier I taught a lesson on discerning the people in your life. If you begin to understand that God allows certain relationships to be severed for purpose, you will also understand which relationships need to be mended and which ones to let go. Does reconciliation mean tea and crumpets with your offender? Not necessarily but, an "I am sorry if I hurt you", goes a long way in the eyes of the Lord. If the outstretched hand and heart are received then you

have gained a brother or a sister, if not then you have done your part and are released of any further obligation to reconcile.

CHAPTER 14

Dis-Empower Your Past

It is so important to finally let the past be the past along with all the things that you have experienced in your past and begin to focus on where you are going. This doesn't mean that we have spiritual amnesia, but it means our past can no longer be a factor in our future other than the use of the lessons that we have learned in the things in which we suffered to build a better future.

The ability for our past to control our now and stake claims in our future must be handed over to who we have become despite our difficulties. We must understand that our existence alone has emancipated us from the strongholds of hurt, disappointment and failure to move on from the frailties of our former selves. The fact that you survived it may often be enough fuel to help you to progress with zeal and determination.

Let's begin to settle our past by making a list of ten (10) things that you have overcome.

_____
_____
_____
_____
_____
_____
_____
_____
_____
_____
_____
_____
_____
_____
_____

From that same list tell why each thing was important for you to overcome.

___

If you are struggling to see yourself a conqueror, then it is time to CHANGE YOUR PROSPECTIVE:

How do you currently see yourself?

___

What strengths do others see in you?

___

What strengths do you see in yourself?

_____
_____
_____
_____
_____

Whatever God has for us is coming out of what we have already been successful in and out of what we have failed in as well. Remember there are no failures, just experiences and life lessons. However it comes after we have become stronger, more powerful, fully developed, matured, and perfected through our successes and failures.

Success isn't about what people say about you, nor is it about how many times you got it right, but it is based on achieving and exceeding your own goals despite disappointments and regrets.

If you have not done so already, start setting goals for your life as benchmarks for where you are currently and for where you are going. Then, strive to achieve more, greater, better, higher over a period of time.

In order to have good success, you must decide on what you want to do with your life and then break the process down into small goals that you can achieve in increments. When you finally achieve those small goals, it will boost your confident to keep on going to the next goal. And remember to celebrate each victory. Don't wait for others to celebrate you, you celebrate you! Once you learn how to celebrate your own successes and failures you will find that you are free of the opinions of people and free from the need to be affirmed by those who have hurt and rejected you over the years.

In order to dis-empower the strongholds of your past, you must first be willing to face the things in your past that you have considered to be failures.

Let's begin with one thing that happened in your past that you know is the greatest hindrance to you moving forward and ask yourself some hard questions.

1. What happened?

2. What are the facts concerning this situation?

3. How did the situation make you feel about yourself?

4. If others were involved, how did the situation make you feel about those who were involved.

5. What assumptions did you make that have not been verified as facts?

6. What are others who love you saying to you about this situation?

7. Do you believe that what they are saying is right or wrong and why?

8. Why is this situation so debilitating to you?

9. What role can you take responsibility for in that situation?

10. If you had a chance to change it, what could you have done differently?

11. What does the word of God say about the situation?

12. What does the word of God say that your response should have been when it happened?

13. What does the word say that your response should be to it in this time in your life?

_____
_____
_____
_____
_____
_____
_____

14. How have you changed since it happened?

_____
_____
_____
_____
_____
_____
_____

15. What did you learn from that situation that you can use as a platform?

_____
_____
_____
_____
_____
_____
_____

The Lord wants us to come alive and not be buried alive in our past traumas.

The future is not determined by your past, but by the actions of your NOW. Ask yourself, "Am I creating something NOW or am I destroying my future because I have not overcome my past.

CHAPTER 15

Breaking Cycles

Cycles are a series of events that are regularly repeated in the same order. Most of us know how certain things are going to play out in our life because we have been down that road before. Often it plays out exactly like we thought it would because our life is stuck in a cycle. This causes us great frustration and makes us feel like things are never going to change.

Cycles are caused by repeated behaviors that are acquired as well as learned behaviors. You learn to act a certain way through your parents, through your environment, at school, at church, etc. You are told don't do this or that, that's not acceptable or that is appropriate behavior. We also learn how to behave through the word of God which often goes against everything we learned from the world.

Over the years we gained so much experience acting a certain way until we have now become experts in our limited behaviors. We know how to do things without conscious thought because these behaviors have now become our nature.

Congratulations! You have now become a product of your behaviors instead of an unlimited man or woman of God who can be everything that you have been created to be. Instead, you have boxed yourselves in to, this is who I am. However, it is not who you are. It is the life that you have designed for yourself through your own behaviors. And yet, you are more than your limited amount of actions and behaviors.

However, breaking these cycles so that our life can be transformed and then expand to greatness, can be challenging to us. Even if you have made up your mind that you have had enough and want different, there has already been a psychological impact on your subconscious mind seared by those same old thoughts that you continue to think.

Your subconscious mind is your inner mind in which the bible calls the reins that interprets and acts upon the predominating thoughts that you continue to think over and over again with your conscious mind. The function of the subconscious mind is to bring into your life circumstances and situations that match what you think. This is how we reap what we sow. Our pattern of thoughts are seeds that are sown into the subconscious mind that impact who we become and produce the life that we live.

The bible says in Mark 4:26-29, *And he said, So is the kingdom of God, as if a man should cast seed (put in or insert) into the ground; And should sleep, and rise night and day, and the seed should spring and grow up, he knoweth not how. For the earth bringeth forth fruit of herself; first the blade, then the ear, after that the full corn in the ear. But when the fruit is brought forth, immediately he putteth in the sickle, because the harvest is come".*

This parable illustrates the power of the subconscious mind to receive the thoughts that we send it, then grow a thought into something that will eventually manifest as the thing that we are constantly thinking on. You think it long enough and it will ultimately become your truth. Remember, the Lord thought everything that there is into existence.

We have that same power to form thoughts that become actions, objects, circumstances and conditions. However, the subconscious mind or the reins, does not discern positive or negative thoughts, but it will receive what you sow into it and produce what it is given.

The Lord said in Jeremiah 17:10, "*I the LORD search the heart, I try the reins, even to give every man according to his ways, and according to the fruit of his doings*".

You must begin to form new thoughts to feed into your subconscious mind in order to break the cycles of your behaviors. Not your own thoughts, but God's word needs to get into your subconscious mind so that your life will change and then advance. David said, try my reins and my heart meaning, try my subconscious and my thoughts. He said, "*Examine me, O LORD, and prove me; try my reins and my heart*". Scrutinize me, inspect all of me closely and thoroughly, test me, investigate my mind (meaning my thoughts and my inmost mind or my subconscious) the deep part of me.

He understood that the hidden part, the secret part, the part of him that must be transformed by his conscious thoughts must be in direct contact and obedience to the word of God.

How can you begin to repair your subconscious so that you can break the cycles and correct the damage done to your life by your thought processes?

1. Recognize your own behavior patterns.
    a. How do you handle situations?
    b. Do you handle them the same every time?
    c. What thoughts do you repeat for an extended period of time?
2. Be accountable, to God first and then to yourself.
    a. Accept responsibility for your way of thinking and your actions.
    b. See how your thoughts produced your circumstances and change!
3. Check your emotions.
    a. Are your emotions leading, or are you spirit-led?
4. Extract the lessons.
    a. What did I learn from that action, or that behavior?
    b. What is God saying to me in it?
    c. Am I willing to do what I know God is saying to me?
    d. Would I rather continue to feed the beast that is me?
5. Make a different choice of behavior than what you would normally make. In unfavorable circumstances, behave unexpectedly. When you do this, everything that is attached to you will begin to shift.

Jesus always chose differently. He never repeated himself, He never repeated his actions because He was greater than one or two actions or behaviors.

CHAPTER 16

Know Your Worth

Worth is the value that a person has considered something to have. And value is the regard that something is held to deserve. Your usefulness, profitability is valuable to others simply because "they" think that you deserve it based on how you make them feel, what you can add to their life, or if you are able to be a benefit to them in some way.

A person's worth is often determined by way of comparison meaning, we determine people's worth based on other people who have similar qualities, looks, gifts, abilities, talents as what you have. If people feel as if they can get the most out of what the other person or people have to offer, then they will devalue you and esteem the other person or people's worth greater than yours. Because they devalue you, then you devalue yourself as if though they are the end all to your identity.

You are also considered to be valuable based on the sum of people with a similar mindset (a group of people who think alike), all of who have concluded that you have little to offer them because you have now become one of millions of counterfeits of one person that was the original just so that you can increase your worth to them.

Many of us have become copy cats, counterfeits trying to replicate someone else's anointing, someone else's life, someone else's gits and purpose. We have wasted valuable time, time that we cannot get back imitating somebody else that we think is more valuable than us. We fail to use that same precious God given time to increase our own value and worth through cultivating our true self.

Who are you? Go ahead, ask yourself.

_____
_____
_____
_____
_____
_____

Now, who are you, really? That is, who has the Lord created you to be with all of your flaws, shortcomings, mistakes, shady past and questionable present?

If we are struggling to answer those questions, then the Lord Himself wants to reveal to us the hidden things concerning our lives. Even though *"the secret things belong to God"*, the bible says that *"the things revealed"*, or the things that are disclosed to us, *"belong to us and to our children that we may do all the words of this law"*.

There is a real difference between what is secret and what is hidden. A secret is unauthorized information that is shared only by a few, it is something that remains beyond understanding or explanation; it is a mystery that God reveals only to those He chooses.

But what is hidden is something that is concealed or difficult to find. If a thing is hidden it is impossible or nearly impossible to see, but it can be found or uncovered by anybody who gains knowledge of its whereabouts or to those who take time and effort to find it. And if it is found or uncovered, it belongs to the one that found it or uncovered it.

With each moment we are given an opportunity to find all of the secrets about us that only the Lord knows, many of which are hidden in plain sight for your protection. If you knew everything about you, then would you be like God? This would be a good discussion topic!

The bible says that you *are "God's workmanship, created in Christ Jesus unto Good works"*. You are God's masterpiece, rare in design and unable to be duplicated and the Lord made you for good works. Good means distinguished or eminent, famous or respected within a sphere or profession.

What is your sphere? What is your area of expertise? Every single one of us has at least one. What is the section of society that you have been called to? Where is your territory?

Find it and work that land.

List below what you believe is/are your area(s) of expertise.

_____
_____
_____
_____
_____
_____
_____
_____
_____
_____

Now list the type (s) of people that you believe that you have been called to.

_____
_____
_____
_____
_____
_____
_____
_____
_____
_____

That word "good" also means renown or known or talked about by many people. The bible says that it was noised that Jesus was in the house. Not because He sent out flyers and had a marketing strategy prior to His arrival, but word got out through word of mouth concerning the good work that He was doing.

What good work(s) have you been performing that you believe that people need to know about that will be of a benefit to them?

The word good also means illustrious, admired or respected for past achievements. Ask yourself, what have you already achieved on your own and not off the back of someone else?

How have you prospered in the things that you have overcome (the situations and circumstances in your life that led others to quit, to give up, to take their own life)?

In what ways did you use your victories to help others?

_____
_____
_____
_____
_____
_____
_____

Based on the answers that you have given, do you believe that you are able to begin to find your true self? Yes or No?

If not, why not?

_____
_____
_____
_____
_____
_____

What would it take for you to discover the real you and the value and worth that is in THAT person?

_____
_____
_____
_____
_____
_____
_____
_____

God has made you to be celebrated by way of the good works that He has already prepared for you to walk in as you make do use of opportunities to be that person that you already are in Him.

Who you are right now is already powerful as proven by the fact that you are still standing. Once you realize the power of survival, you will begin to use your survival story as a launching pad to the masses.

Begin to tell yourself, I have power, I am strong, I can prevail, I can be whole, I can be a force.

Affirmations are not a new thing. They began when God saw all that He created and said, "It is very good". An affirmation is the action or process of affirming something or stating something as being a fact. The fact is "I can do". It is not, "can I do".

How often do we place our own worth in others? If they think we are important, then we think that we are important. If others celebrate us, then we feel accomplished. If someone is pushing us to keep going, then we keep pressing.

But, what do you do when you find yourself all alone with no one to motivate you? You motivate yourself!

King David, had to motivate himself through sorrow, disbelief and probably even a questioning of his calling and his abilities in the Lord when his men spoke of stoning him because of their tremendous loss as Ziklag. However, the bible says that David *"encouraged himself in the Lord"*. The bible does not say exactly what he did or said at that time, however based on so many passages in the book of Psalms that were written by David, we can assume that David reminded himself of the battles that he already won in the Lord and of the anointing that was on his life as King of Israel.

David said, in Psalms 139:14, *"I will praise thee; for I am fearfully and wonderfully made: marvellous are thy works; and that my soul knoweth right well"*. He said, Lord, you made me to be held in awe, and you made me to be extraordinary and marvelous and every fiber of my being greatly knows this about myself.

Not only did David know that he was made to be honored and respected and that he was different than anyone else that was ever created, but he was confident of these facts. David affirmed himself by saying I am extraordinary, I am not mediocre or normal, but I am great!

When you become confident in your own self, others will feed off that same confidence that you have in your own abilities and be drawn to you through the good work that you were created to do.

It is important that you stop seeing the things that you overcame as mistakes and failures but see them as accomplishment and triumphs so that you can boost your self-confidence.

Self-confidence is your own assessment of your own abilities and the power that is at work in you based on the experiences that you have already overcome and conquered.

Take a real long assessment of your life and remember all of the things that you have survived, the things that you have lived through, the mountains that you have come over and the hardships that you have already endured and know that if you made it through that, you can make it through anything.

CHAPTER 17

See The Beauty In Your Scars

Wounds are caused by injuries that penetrate the skin which in the spirit realm is representative of our flesh which includes our feelings, our emotions, how we think and act outside of the controlling of the Holy Spirit.

Paul told his fellow shipmates; *Sirs I perceive that this voyage will be with hurt and much damage not only of the lading and ship but also of our lives.*

Many, if not most of us will be hurt, wounded, injured, not just a physical injury, but mental injury, injury inflicted by the violence of the storms of this life. You will be harmed, you will suffer reproach. You will be wounded, disappointed, there will be some things that happen to you that you will disapprove of and there will be loss, so much loss. You will also suffer detriment, you will at times be impaired, put at a disadvantage. You will be made to feel like people have done a disservice to you. You will experience being wronged and treated unkindly. But if you stay with the ship (your mission. purpose and assignment), your life will be saved.

However, if you stay, you will also have to live with the scars of what you have been through for the sake of that mission, purpose, and assignment. But I love this, a scar is a natural part of the healing process.

Scars are the marks left by a "healed" wound. Wound healing comes in stages and what the scar looks like, will determine if the wound has been completely healed. Meaning, how you act after it is over will determine if you have been completely healed.

Many are yet trying to function through life with unhealed wounds. When the wound is not attended to, it seeps and depending on how fresh the wound is, it may still seep blood. The man found by the good Samaritan was freshly wounded, therefore his wounds could be bandaged up and he sent on his way.

But many of us have been left by the roadside and passed over by people on their way to their own destiny and have been left with wounds that have become infected. When a wound is infected it becomes even more tender to the touch. This is why so many people are sensitive about certain things in their life, things that are now touchy subjects.

But when the wound has been completely healed, you don't mind saying "Oh, this happened to me, but God. If it wasn't for Jesus, I would not have survived that". When you have been completely healed, you no longer worry about hiding or covering up those areas, because you know that was in the past.

When Jesus encountered His disciples after His resurrection, He wasn't trying to hide his scars. As a matter of fact, He told Thomas, look at my hands and see the scars, thrust your hand into my side. Scars are identifying marks, features that show who someone is. Thomas would not have believed it was Jesus except for the scars!

There is a story behind each one of your scars. You fell off the bicycle as a child, you cut yourself on a piece of glass, you were in a serious accident. And yet, each time you were healed, and the scar is the proof that it happened and that you are better now.

Scars are what you see when you look at yourself and what other's see when they look at you and these are very often two different views. In your mind they are imperfections, I was abused, molested, abandoned, left for dead. But to other's they characterize you. People now see you helping battered women, see you ministering to addicts, to wayward children and they want to know how you came to have such love and compassion for others.

It is the scars caused by the wounds that distinguish you and set you apart for purpose.

Many spend a lifetime trying to cover up scars and trying to mask the pain of life's experiences. We spend time trying to hide our scars with make-up, long pants, long sleeves because we have been made to think that scars are ugly. We want to have an outwardly perfect experience in this life as if we have never been through anything, however people see you and know that the only way that you can be that perfect is if you are covering something up.

Stop hiding what you have overcome. Throughout eternity Jesus will have nail scarred hands and feet to prove that He is the Christ. Your scars are proof that you are who the Lord called you to be and that you have successfully completed the mission despite the pain, the suffering and all the life lessons that you struggled to learn.

You are beautiful and uniquely designed through pain.

www.ingramcontent.com/pod-product-compliance
Lightning Source LLC
Chambersburg PA
CBHW080404170426
43193CB00016B/2811